IN THE MEANTIME

IN THE MEANTIME

OWN YOUR FINANCIAL NARRATIVE

SHEHARA L. WOOTEN, CFP®

NEW DEGREE PRESS
COPYRIGHT © 2021 SHEHARA L. WOOTEN
All rights reserved.

IN THE MEANTIME
OWN YOUR FINANCIAL NARRATIVE

ISBN   978-1-63730-439-6 *Paperback*
        978-1-63730-535-5 *Kindle Ebook*
        978-1-63730-536-2 *Ebook*

To God, for He is faithful.

*To my husband, Sean, for your
ongoing support and love.*

*To my mom and dad, Harry and Debra,
for your encouragement and wisdom.*

CONTENTS

INTRODUCTION   1

SECTION 1. BUILD   11

CHAPTER 1.   UNDERSTANDING YOUR VALUES   13

CHAPTER 2.   TENACITY   25

CHAPTER 3.   NET WORTH   37

SECTION 2. LIVE   49

CHAPTER 4.   THE BETTER RAINY DAYS: SAVINGS AND EMERGENCY FUND   53

CHAPTER 5.   PROTECT YOUR WEALTH: ARE YOU ON TEAM "BOUNCE MY LAST CHECK?"   67

SECTION 3. SAVE   79

CHAPTER 6.   DON'T PUT ALL YOUR MONEY IN ONE BUCKET   81

CHAPTER 7.   OWE NO MAN: FROM DEBT MANAGEMENT TO DEBT ELIMINATION   89

CHAPTER 8.   START WITH WHAT YOU HAVE   99

SECTION 4. GIVE **113**

CHAPTER 9. YOUR FINANCIAL SUCCESS STORY 115

CHAPTER 10. THE CAPACITY TO GIVE 133

CHAPTER 11. COMMUNITY 143

CONCLUSION 153

RESOURCES 157

ACKNOWLEDGMENTS 159

APPENDIX 161

INTRODUCTION

"They took a huge axe and started whacking at my sister Aileen's beloved piano—whack, whack, whack! It was a good piano. And they thought that was something we shouldn't have," recalls Olive J. Hooker, who was six years old when the Tulsa Race Massacre occurred. She recounts this part of her experience at 103 years old (Rao 2018).

Many start with the Tulsa "Race Massacre" of 1921 in telling the story of "Black Wall Street." "Black Wall Street" in the Greenwood District of Tulsa, Oklahoma, was considered one of the most affluent Black communities in the United States at the time (Clark 2021). Although the cruel incident was deemed a riot, it should be categorized as a massacre, as this thriving section of Tulsa was destroyed out of pure evil, jealousy, and terror during the Jim Crow Era. The massacre claimed the lives of at least three hundred people, mostly Black lives, after a white mob attacked the community and burned it to the ground in approximately twenty-four hours starting on May 31, 1921 and ending on June 1, 1921 (Astor 2020).

There were approximately six thousand to ten thousand displaced residents of Greenwood who were housed in internment camps following the massacre (Morrison 2021). According to the Oklahoma Historical Society, survivors were forced to work in these internment camps and "the mayor threatened to arrest anyone refusing to work for vagrancy." No one remained in the camps by the middle of June.

Life after the massacre was extremely hard for the survivors. They lost everything: their homes, livelihood, churches, and businesses. The reason for calling the massacre a riot was so that victims could not make insurance claims. Riots would not provide a payout, but a massacre would. The damage to this burned-down section of Tulsa, Oklahoma was an estimated total property loss of $2 million, which equates to over $50 million to $200 million (Gara 2020 and Henderson 2020).

The visionary behind the origins of the Greenwood district is rarely discussed. His name was O. W. Gurley, an Arkansas native and wealthy Black landowner. He was born on Christmas day in 1868 to freed enslaved Africans in Huntsville, Alabama. He was self-educated and, after marrying his childhood sweetheart, Emma, he decided to pursue his dream of a better life. Thus, he risked all that he had to join "the homesteaders seeking freedom, opportunity and wealth in the Great Oklahoma Land Rush." (Moreno 2019)

At the age of twenty-five in 1893, he and Emma staked a claim on a plot of land that became known as Perry, Oklahoma, which was one of many towns advertised to Blacks in this territory. Gurley was ambitious, and after hearing that there was an opportunity to strike oil, he wanted to seize it. In 1905, he sold his land in Perry, Oklahoma, and moved to Tulsa, purchasing forty acres of land. Along with his decision to purchase the land, he committed to only sell the land to Black settlers.

His first business was a rooming house located on a dusty trail near railroad tracks. He named the road Greenwood Avenue after a town in Mississippi, giving the Greenwood district its namesake. Many Black Americans heard about the area and began moving to Greenwood, hoping to leave the oppression they experienced in the Jim Crow South. In November 1905, a discovery well drilled twelve miles southwest of Tulsa secured the city's right to claim the title, "Oil Capital of the World." That oil strike was the first of several oil strikes contributing to Tulsa's prosperity (Energy HQ 2017). As Tulsa, Oklahoma thrived, Mr. Gurley's Greenwood thrived along with it.

According to Hannibal Johnson, author of *Black Wall Street: From Riot to Renaissance in Tulsa's Historic Greenwood District*, O. W. Gurley is credited with having the first Black business in Greenwood. Hannibal Johnson writes, "He envisioned creating something for Black people by Black people." In keeping with his vision, Mr. Gurley would even loan money to people who wanted to start businesses, allowing them to experience the same opportunities as he did.

"Oklahoma banned Black men from working in the oil fields, but Black men and women could earn a decent living performing service jobs, such as working as maids, groundskeepers, seamstresses, and food servers" (Moreno 2019). Due to segregation laws and oppression, the businesses built from Greenwood were created from necessity and for survival. Between 1910 and 1920, the population of Tulsa rose from less than two thousand to almost nine thousand (Gara 2020). By 1920, "Black Wall Street" was more than thirty-five city blocks of luxury shops, restaurants, grocery stores, hotels, jewelry and clothing stores, salons, libraries, movie theaters, night clubs, pool halls, doctors, dentists, and lawyer offices.

The residents of Greenwood are incredible, especially given they were enslaved fifty years prior with no help from the US government and created thriving, self-sustaining, and self-reliant communities. The power of community economics was truly at play in Greenwood. Many resources state that the dollar circulated within the Greenwood community nineteen to one hundred times. According to an article in the *Atlanta Black Star*, the dollar may have remained in the community for about a year. In contrast, today the dollar remains in the Black community for about six hours according to the NAACP (Montford 2014).

There are numerous stories of the wealth attained and accumulated from "Black Wall Street." O. W. Gurley was one of many who attained wealth in the Greenwood District. Another contemporary of O. W. Gurley was J. B. Stradford, a lawyer and activist born into the enslavement in Kentucky. Stradford believed Black people had a better chance of economic progress if they pooled their resources. He opened the largest Black-owned hotel in the United States, called the Stradford Hotel. He also owned large tracts of land in the northeastern part of Tulsa and sold the land exclusively to Black Americans.

O. W. Gurley was extremely ambitious and continued to expand. He owned and rented three brick apartment buildings, five townhouses, and a grocery store. Gurley's portfolio was estimated to be worth more than $150,000 at that time, which equates to about $5 million today (Gara 2020). Unfortunately, Gurley lost all his wealth when his property was burnt to the ground during the 1921 Race Massacre. Estimates state that more than $200 million dollars of damage occurred due to the massacre (Henderson 2020).

The destruction of Greenwood is a thorough example and case study as to why the 228-year wealth gap exists today. As noted previously, the estimated damages would be equivalent to $200 million in today's dollars, but the cost was higher because when generational wealth is passed on, it gets the opportunity to compound and thus expand exponentially, as noted by John W. Rogers, Jr., chairman of Ariel Investments and great grandson of J. B. Stradford (Gara 2020). Even though the Black community has come to find that as they take two steps forward, they are pushed a step or two or three back, we continue to strive as we find innovative ways to create generational wealth and break through economic injustice. We are resilient.

People often assume that "Black Wall Street" worked because it attracted great people, but the reality is the community worked because of the community. I want to dispel the notion that one must pull themselves up by their own bootstraps. I wondered if there were ways to create similar community-powered wealth through actions today, and what I have found has given me a new picture of the future of wealth creation. In this book, I will explore the intersection of the racial wealth gap and empowering stories of those men and women who were able to overcome systemic challenges to create their personal definition of wealth just like Gurley, Stradford, and countless others from "Black Wall Street." One example of how this concept still continues today is that Dr. Michael Carter, Sr., a theologian who in 1998 founded Black Wall Street USA, a nonprofit organization created "to establish urban economic districts and commercial centers where at least 50 percent of businesses are owned by Black people," according to an *Inc Magazine* article entitled "Meet the Entrepreneur Who Created the First 'Black Wall Street'"

(Henderson 2020). According to Songfacts, even The Gap Band was originally called "Greenwood, Archer, and Pine Street Band" in honor of their Tulsa Roots.

I want readers to understand that this collection of inspiring stories has a prevailing theme: some way, somehow, someone has helped these successful people achieve greatness on their journey to wealth accumulation. Contrary to popular belief, it takes community—a community of like-minded individuals on seemingly separate paths coming together to create and make their financial dreams come true. No one does this as an island. For Greenwood to thrive, people had to patronize and make purchases from those in their community. No one makes it by themselves. It takes collaboration.

I believe the collection of inspirational stories is the start for you to have your own "super" community so to speak. "Your network is your net worth." The stories in this book will be your "super" network. Although you may never meet these folks in person, you can use their stories as motivation to strive, to thrive, and to aspire to be the best person you were created to be. Not only will inspiring stories be interwoven into this book, but I will also discuss financial literacy concepts and provide exercises at the end of each chapter, entitled "Action Provoking Exercise," which will allow you to implement some of the ideas presented as you read along. You may also go to the Resources section at the end of the book to download a free Companion Workbook.

Although many people will glean solid information from reading this book, it is mainly speaking to Black Americans who want to change the trajectory of their financial future. There are four sections in this book: Section 1: Build, Section 2: Live, Section 3: Save, and Section 4: Give. I'm looking forward to sharing some financial principles in each section as well as inspiring stories of those who have experienced success against all odds. They didn't do it alone, and you shouldn't either.

I came from humble beginnings myself. As a child, I observed my parents working hard to provide a great life for my sisters and me. Both of my parents grew up poor. They knew that hard work, education, and determination would get us beyond what even their parents achieved. They made sure I knew and took pride in my Black history. They made sure I understood the resiliency of my ancestors and how it runs through my DNA. Once I realized my potential, I worked hard to achieve the best grades that I could so that I could walk in the excellence instilled by my parents.

Growing up, I remember my mother going through several company mergers, which threatened her employment. It was always scary to me that a company could give you a pink slip, and before you know it, you're laid off with no job. Thank God she was able to keep her job, though. She retired from her company after more than forty years of service. My father worked a full-time job for the state, and although it was considered to be pretty safe, he was determined to have multiple streams of income. When I was in high school, he started his tax preparation business, which is still in operation today. He also pursued real estate and created a real estate portfolio that worked for him and my mother. From observing their experiences, I knew that my path would eventually lead to entrepreneurship. I knew that I couldn't rely on a corporation's loyalty to me and felt working for a company the rest of my life would be riskier than starting a business in the long run.

A few years after earning my BS in electrical and computer engineering, I decided to change careers and become a financial advisor. Like most endeavors, my path to becoming an entrepreneur and financial planner had its twists and turns. After graduating college, I became interested in personal finances after having a not-so-great experience with a financial advisor at twenty-five years old. I started to read and study personal finance and applied these exciting new concepts to my own life. I found that I made great strides and decided to pursue financial planning as a career. In 2004, I officially changed careers and, by 2016, I started my own firm called Your Story Financial, LLC, to help professionals move from unsure about their finances to confident about their money so that they can create their own narrative of what financial freedom means to them.

Unfortunately, none of the members of the white mob were ever convicted of a crime. Their descendants are reaping the benefits of the land they stole. On the other hand, the survivors of the massacre, as well as their descendants, never received any restitution or reparations. Although this book focuses more on what we can do as Black Americans to create a strong financial future, my hope is that we can start the reparations process with finally getting justice for the descendants of the residents of Black Wall Street and, sadly, other cities like Rosewood, Florida, Elaine, Arkansas, Slocum, Texas, and Wilmington, North Carolina, just to name a few of too many. Once the descendants of Greenwood receive reparations, then my hope is that all descendants of Enslaved Africans in the U.S. will get reparations.

Economic injustice and systemic racism's role in the racial wealth gap must be rectified. The systems of economic injustice, from 246 years of the cruel and violent enslavement in the US to the continuation of terrorism toward the Black community through the Jim Crow era and today, must be rectified and repaired. In the meantime, I hope this book serves as a resource for those who want to change the trajectory of wealth for their family for generations to come and close this racial wealth gap until economic justice is served and reparations are paid.

SECTION 1

BUILD

> "It's not how much money you make, but how much money you keep, how hard it works for you, and how many generations you keep it for."
>
> —ROBERT KIYOSAKI

There's an old saying that goes, "Money doesn't grow on trees," but I remember coming across the saying, "Let your money grow like trees." Wouldn't it be great if our money could grow like a tree? One thing about a tree is that it starts as a seed. A seed is very small but powerful. "A typical seed includes three basic parts: (1) an embryo, (2) a supply of nutrients for the embryo, and (3) a seed coat" (Kiddie Encyclopedia 2021). The part of the seed that stands out the most to me is the supply of nutrients for the embryo. Just like a seed, we need to start somewhere with growing our money and get our supply of nutrients to help nourish it so that it can continue to grow.

If someone has a goal to reach $1,000,000 in net worth, it starts with that first investment. To reach a net worth of $1,000,000, you have to ask yourself some questions. What amount should I start out with? How long will I give myself to reach $1,000,000? How frequently will I add to the accounts?

When it comes to our money and investing, we must be patient. Over time an investment will reap rewards. A tree grows in all its majesty from a small seed to a sapling to a beautiful green life-giving structure. Money must start small and grow over time. There's no getting rich quick with investing.

Be encouraged that if you are eliminating debt, you are on the road to growth because every dollar you put toward your debt lowers the balance that is accumulating interest. Your money may not be growing in the traditional sense but it's getting closer to the positive.

Even if you are not in debt, if you are focused on increasing your income, you're giving your money an opportunity to grow. Make sure you are getting paid what you are worth and make sure that you seek out ways to have additional income sources. I am a proponent of the idea that single people as well as married couples should have multiple income sources. Just like when we invest we shouldn't put all our eggs in one basket, we shouldn't have one income source either. I will discuss that further in future chapters.

In this section, we'll also cover the power of growing in your grasp of financial information. This is an area that will reap benefits for a long time and allow you to take action so that you are not intimidated by financial information.

CHAPTER 1

UNDERSTANDING YOUR VALUES

"… we as a nation must undergo a radical revolution of values. We must rapidly begin the shift from a 'thing-oriented' society to a 'person-oriented' society. When machines and computers, profit motives and property rights are considered more important than people, the giant triplets of racism, materialism, and militarism are incapable of being conquered…"

—DR. MARTIN LUTHER KING, JR.

Martin Luther King, Jr., said we must shift from a "thing-oriented" society to a "person-oriented" society. Our values are our guiding force, and by knowing our values and making financial decisions in line with our values, we can alleviate stress and anxiety. I am reminded how important it is to become connected to your values, especially with money. For instance, if you value security and don't have an emergency fund, then every time life happens and you have an unexpected circumstance that will require money, you may get stressed at the thought of having to figure out how you will pay for this emergency.

According to a survey produced by Capital One, "Seventy-seven percent of Americans are anxious about their financial situation, fifty-eight percent feel their finances control their lives rather than the other way around, and fifty-two percent have difficulty controlling money-related worries" (Gaetano 2020).

Although money cannot buy happiness, "Research has shown that our day-to-day happiness generally tends to scale with our incomes until we hit a wall around the $75,000 mark. The study noted that, up to this point, it's not so much that the money makes us happy by itself but, rather, it better staves off the things that make us unhappy. People below this $75,000 mark feel more grounded by the problems they already have while those with incomes at or above it can avoid everyday stresses" (Gaetano 2020, and Luscombe 2010).

I believe the statistics above show why so many people have a love-hate relationship with money. Some feel that money is evil, and others feel money is everything. The statistics above provide some balance and harmony as for the purpose of money.

Paradigm Shift to Money as a Tool

Money is a tool to be used for a greater purpose. Rha Goddess's story from her TED Talk, "Born to Move the Crowd," exemplifies that. Rha Goddess was a starving artist and then woke up. As the daughter of Ruth and Fred, who survived over two decades of Jim Crow Era segregation, she was born at the "intersection of civil rights and hip hop." Her parents taught her at a very young age to share, and she says, "… we understood that those who were less fortunate were no different than us. And it was only by the grace of God that the shoe was not on the other foot." She respected the values her parents instilled in her and how the civil rights movement made strides.

However, by her mid-teens, she became "frustrated and impatient with the civil rights movement." Most likely her frustration stemmed from the concern that strides and changes were taking too long. She would find herself expressing her rage in writing hip-hop lyrics for hours in her bedroom. However, the local "cyphas" only allowed for the boys to take center stage. A "cypha," or cypher, is a term "Used when a group of rappers, typically standing in a circle, would take turns exchanging verses for competition, practice or sheer entertainment" (Pullum 2019). One day she heard Sha-Rock, a female rapper from the legendary group Funky Four Plus One More. She was mesmerized by Sha-Rock's style. To her delight, Sha-Rock invited Rha Goddess to get off the sidelines and participate in rapping.

She became more and more involved in hip-hop and received the opportunity to travel the world. Her motivation was to make a difference in the lives of others using hip-hop to unify and to bring out the best in the crowds she performed for. As hip-hop evolved, she saw that by the mid '90s, hip-hop culture "began to call me names that brought tears to my eyes." In this statement she was referencing the way in which women were treated. Capitalism had found a new art form created to edify a people and used it for the production of "money, power, and respect by any means necessary." "Hip hop had lost its way from being a conscious art form and elevating the community to being a money making machine that idolized gang banging boys and hyper sexualized girls."

When I heard Rha Goddess's story, I couldn't help but recall the lyrics to the song "What They Do" by The Roots. The Roots is one of my favorite rap groups, and I feel they achieved the balance between entertainment and conscious rap. I remember in the late '90s to early 2000s when "What They Do" came out. All the other rap videos showed rappers surrounded by scantily clad women and well-dressed men covered in gold chains and designer clothing in luxury vehicles. The song "What They Do" dispelled the myth that these video scenes were real. Many of those videos glorified the opulence but the rappers in the videos were most likely renting these material items to look as if they were living a life of luxury. Hearing Rha Goddess's story made me think of this song because she committed to avoiding what wasn't in line with her values and only following her chief core values.

She said, "I took the high road of becoming a hip-hop cultural purist. And I ignored capitalism, [and] said it didn't matter." I am inspired by her journey from what she shares as ignoring capitalism to waking up to find her footing in it.

Her turning point was coming back from an international trip. As she puts it, she was "broke and had no clue how I was going to pay the rent." She resolved that she wasn't going to scramble anymore to figure it out.

From that point forward she had several come-to-Jesus moments. She recognized a few things:

> "I had developed a hip-hop purist persona and romanticized the culture to the point that in its current state it would take us to the promised land." However,

hip-hop purists like herself didn't have the "emotional, spiritual, nor financial capacity to pull it off."

She "found herself consistently engaging under-resourced communities who had tremendous amounts of need." She realized she had "to own all of the places where I said yes to my own exploitation. Overworked, underpaid and mildly appreciated was my norm."

She had to own that despite all her judgement of those "commercial rappers," she was just like them. She still used hip-hop to get ahead, but they had more in their bank accounts. As the "righteous rapper," she had worn the starving artist badge proudly for over fifteen years. She was done with that. She learned that her "why" was bigger than hip-hop, and it was about being on the front lines of humanity.

She decided "to slow down, get real, woman up, and figure out the money."

From there, she got a business education. She didn't go to the Ivy League schools or even a state school for that matter. She decided to sit at the feet of some multi-millionaires who had a repeated track record of building successful businesses. She learned about money, making money, her relationship with money, and what it meant to actually have money be a part of her life. She learned all that she could from them.

However, she needed to marry her creative side to her values and her experiences as a Black woman, which were at the center of all her decisions. She couldn't start her real entrepreneurial journey until she reconciled her relationship with capitalism. She realized that capitalism was about competition, meaning who was better and who was worse, who was a winner and who was a loser, what was good and what was bad. She rejected this notion and didn't embrace what she called the culture of capitalism, a culture subscribing to the notion that there isn't enough. It thrives on scarcity.

However, as the "righteous rapper," she hadn't put anything in the place of her thought on capitalism thriving on scarcity or competition. She had to replace her mindset about the culture of capitalism as she knew it by creating a new vision for wealth. She could no longer put the responsibility of her piety on "the system." She had to be 100 percent responsible for her experience.

This was difficult for her because her previous mindset led her to believe that everything she experienced was due to external forces. But that isn't so. It's your potential inside. I like to think that God has given us all an assignment, and it's our job to ask Him what that assignment is. How can I discover it? How do I maximize it, despite the outside forces such as systemic racism and lack of reparations from the US or any other challenges coming against your assignment? Rha decided to really dig into herself and discover what she wanted to do. So she created a mantra: "Stay true, get paid, do good." Today, Rha Goddess is an author and a life coach who provides consulting services as well as online courses to entrepreneurs and leaders. Rha Goddess is a shining example of introspectively confirming our core values and the part they play in all our life decisions—including money decisions.

I love that she was able to interweave her true authentic self with making a great living. This resonated with me because I changed careers to help people. In 2009, I worked with a company that got me closer to my goal of helping people by creating a business model where I could become a financial advisor and work with individuals and families. I worked hard. In fact, I was known as the hardest worker. One year I even received an award entitled "Who you most likely will find at work on a Friday night at 6 p.m."—something to that effect. I appreciated the recognition and knew that it wasn't true that I'd be found there on a Friday night, but you'd find me there any other night from Monday through Thursday (except Wednesday, since I made sure to attend weekly Bible study).

In the course of my journey, I saw so many other financial advisors passing me by, and I knew something was wrong with this picture. That's when I decided that the business model no longer served me, and it didn't allow me to serve my clients to the fullest extent that I wanted to serve them. This was recently confirmed when I received more evidence from a former client I was helping. You see, I never charged this client because the business model at the time didn't make room for charging her for the specific services she needed at that time. I didn't want to sell her a product that didn't fit her needs.

Before starting my own firm, I would provide free advice because I knew it was best for the client. This former client decided she wanted to work with me again because she wanted to save more. She said that I helped her get on track five years ago and that she was so happy she followed my advice and made changes. Now she's coming to me, and I have a model that will charge her fairly, so we both win. To have her share with me that my advice had made such an impact makes me feel so good. However, going forward I decided not to do that for free. It's important to have an honest look at our thinking about money, how we've come to develop our perspective on it, and how it has guided our lives and financial decisions.

Our Values as a Guide

Our values are our guide and give us the conviction that we need to stay focused on whatever we endeavor to accomplish. Raven Magwood is a brilliant example. She is from South Carolina and is an author, motivational speaker, accomplished gymnast, and business owner. According to a podcast interview on *Black Wealth Renaissance*, at twelve years old she published her first book, was a freshman in high school, and gave her first speech for Stedman Graham. Her journey and life goal are to inspire people. She graduated from high school at sixteen years old and started college. She attended Clemson University at nineteen years old and, after graduation, she started filming her first movie. Everything she does is with the goal to have people walk away a better person. In terms of values, she lives her life by the quote, "My life may be the only Bible that another person reads."

Her teacher gave her the motivation to write her first book. At the time, she was a national gymnastic champion and had skipped two grades. Her book ended up helping her to display not only her successes but her setbacks and failures. She is now twenty-six years old, and the book that she wrote at such a young age is still being used by elementary schools to this day.

She confirmed that the book she wrote was an impactful book when, after she gave a speech, a forty-year-old man with tears in his eyes told her that he had attempted suicide three times in his life and was planning to commit suicide that day. After seeing a twelve-year-old so passionate and positive about life, he said, he would never attempt to take his life again. This situation gave her the conviction to continue to motivate and inspire people with her work. When she was about to graduate from college, she realized that she could monetize her interest in motivating and inspiring people. She started charging her worth for speeches and selling more books to make a living from what she loved doing.

Raven advises that in order to make a living doing what you love, you must "find the intersection of your passion and what you like to do and how you can fulfill a need, and that's how you'll make money doing something you really enjoy."

Raven had a wonderful support system in her parents. Her mother is very good with money. She also read *Rich Dad Poor Dad*, which opened her eyes to the importance of assets and creating "cashflow in a way that you'll be set for life, so to speak." Although she was at the center of these accomplishments, she didn't do this in a vacuum. She had a solid community.

Now, Raven owns a gymnastics training business. She went from coaching at the gym after school to being offered the opportunity to buy the gym from the owner after a few years. The owner felt she made such an impact on the girls in the gym that he wanted to sell it to her when he retired. She decided to move forward with purchasing the gym by partnering with her mother on the venture, and the gym has made record profits. She is not only a gym owner, but she still coaches and mentors the girls. She is a big fan of being open to opportunities as they come along and listening to God's nudge to move forward.

In addition to owning a gym, she is writing screen plays for filming and making movies. She loves creating and making things. She is not a formally trained screenwriter, as she learned how to write screen plays via Google research. Her first film wasn't very popular, but it was fun for her and won film festival awards (Bellard 2020, and Brook 2019).

A prevailing theme for both Rha Goddess and Raven is that they pursued opportunities that were in line with their values. Again, our values are our guiding force in how we make our decisions, especially our money decisions.

Now, it's your turn. At the end of every chapter, I've included an "Action Provoking Exercise." The exercise will help you to consider what you've read and how you may implement the concepts shared.

Action Provoking Exercise

What are your Core Values? Circle at least three of your top Core Values. You may add to the list below if there's a value that is not listed that describes you.

Independence	**Accountability**
Honesty	**Charity**
Integrity	**Hard Work**
Creativity	**Optimism**
Efficiency	**Friendship**
Reliability	**Self-care**
Discipline	**Wealth**
Family	**Leisure**
Diligence	**Fun**
Resilience	**Service**
Abundance	**Leaving a Legacy**
Security	

- What stood out to you about the values that you chose?
- Are they aligned with how you make your financial decisions?
- If not, what do you need to do to make sure they are aligned?
- For example, if you chose security but you don't have an emergency fund, how can you make sure that you make progress toward starting an emergency fund?

CHAPTER 2

TENACITY

"Many of life's failures are people who did not realize how close they were to success when they gave up."
—THOMAS A. EDISON

The fact that I am here today and that we are all here is powerful and profound. I mustn't take this for granted because my ancestors have survived so that I can be here today. *Finding Your Roots*, a television show hosted by Henry "Skip" Louis Gates, Jr. that I thoroughly enjoy, tells the stories of the ancestors of its guests, who are well-known movie stars or prominent public figures. This show inspires me in so many ways. Professor Gates takes each guest through various facts and stories about their ancestors, whether they were fleeing persecution to have a better life in America to surviving the Middle Passage and enduring brutal inhumane conditions. I think, "Wow, I'm here because of my Black ancestors' tenacity."

Tenacity and determination are driving forces that we as humans have to achieve our purpose and goals.

When I was a child, I remember expressing an interest in a speech competition. I was only eight years old and in third grade. I mentioned it to my teacher, and she shared it with the school principal. I distinctly remember my principal calling me out of the classroom to share with me that she thought that I was too shy for a speech competition, and I shouldn't participate. I was amazed that she would tell me this. When I came home from school, I told my mother. She asked me if it's something I would like to do. I told her yes. From that point forward, we started practicing for the competition.

I ended up competing, and it was a total disaster. I completely forgot my speech. I was memorizing Isaiah 53. I wasn't too far into my presentation when I started fumbling over my words and completely mixed up all the scriptures. I looked out into the crowd of judges and could see the pity in their faces. I completed the speech and received a participant's ribbon. The participant ribbon was basically a "thank you for joining us today." I felt bad for a moment and briefly remembered the empty words of my school principal, but when the next opportunity to compete came along, I jumped on it. This time I was in fifth or seventh grade, and I was ten or twelve years old. I ended up practicing as much as I could. I even had a trial run in front of my classmates. This time I flopped during the practice run in front of my classmates, too. I sat down and thought, "Oh no, this will not happen again."

By the time of the competition, I was able to compete and earned a superior rating. From that point forward, I competed in additional speech competitions, and in high school I joined the speech and debate team and ended up making it to the state competition in my junior and senior years of high school. I don't know what made me so interested in giving speeches at a young age, but I do know that God's divine providence was at work. I now use speaking as a part of my work and enjoy giving presentations and conducting workshops to this day. If I had given up at the point of failure, I would not have been able to attain this useful skill set.

I believe this determination and tenacity is ever so required when it comes to focusing on our financial goals. Whether it's learning a new aspect of financial education like investing, budgeting, developing your money mindset, etc., it's so important to be determined to reach your financial goals—even when it's tough and even when you don't get it right the first time.

Arian Simone and Trey Brown are two people that come to mind when I think of tenacity. Their stories of triumph in the midst of challenges are so inspiring. Both are creating empires because they have a drive. Their tenacity is helping them create financial legacies for themselves and their families.

Arian Simone

Arian Simone was a born entrepreneur from childhood. She even sold Mary Kay, a make up and skin care brand that is sold by individual consultants through direct selling efforts, which is a difficult way to start a business. She was born to an upper-middle-class family in east Detroit and started paying her own bills at an early age. However, her parents never taught her about money. She learned that from life experiences.

As I continued to watch the YouTube video entitled "Arian Simone's Fearless Journey," I concluded that to say Arian is a go-getter is an understatement. She owned a boutique in the mall while attending college. After raising a couple hundred thousand for her boutique—yes, I said about $200,000—she found herself sitting on the floor in her new boutique and said to herself that one day she was going to be the investor that she was looking for. At the time she knew nothing about investors, venture capitalists, or anything of that sort. She just knew that she would help to fund business and invest in entrepreneurs.

She ended up graduating from Florida A&M in Tallahassee, Florida, and moved to LA to start her new job at Apple Bottoms. With this new job, she was expecting stability. I imagine that she saw nothing but success ahead of her. To her dismay, after working there for thirty days and gaining some momentum, she was laid off. Not too long after, she ran out of money and went from living in her apartment to living in her car. She was homeless for seven months.

Times became extremely desperate, and she started selling her own clothes so she could eat and put gas in the tank. At one point, her car broke down and she needed to live in a shelter. She even lived with friends, but they ended up getting kicked out of their apartment, too.

Through it all, she was in good spirits most of the time. To stay motivated, she would drive through Beverly Hills and look at the houses and the luxurious cars. She was encouraged for the most part. Seeing these affluent neighborhoods encouraged her and was a reminder that some day she could live in a neighborhood like this.

Then, one day, she broke down crying to her mother out of sheer exhaustion and depression from all her life challenges. She said she wasn't suicidal, but she did call her mom in a pool of tears saying, "If this is what life looks like, I don't see a need to live." She was tired of being broke, tired of selling her clothes just to get a meal. This hardship took a toll on her. Normally, she would have called her parents for money, but they were in a divorce case at the time, so she couldn't call them for financial support on this occasion.

Eventually, someone called her to do some PR marketing work, and at that point she had gone seven days without food. She was desperate to say the least. Her first client referred her to someone else who then referred her to someone else, and in about two weeks she had five to seven projects. However, due to her homelessness, she needed to find a place to meet her clients. Unfortunately, she couldn't afford both an office and an apartment.

Even though Arian was in desperate times, she seemed to always realize that she wasn't alone. She still leveraged her network and community. Fortunately, she was able to get office space through her sorority sister and located her company at 5900 Wilshire on the twenty-sixth floor. She was able to reach out to her sorority sister for help. When we are in seemingly hopeless situations, the question to ask is, "How can I get out of this and who do I know that can help?" We can't be so ashamed that we don't ask for assistance. She decided to make this new office space her home and her office. Although she was living in her office, it had no showers, so she took her showers at the LA Fitness, on the first floor of her office building. To her advantage, at the time, Steve Harvey's radio show, on the radio station 100.3 The Beat, was on the nineteenth floor of 5900 Wilshire.

Arian had a plan. Since all her normal resources were no longer available to bail her out, she resolved to call on God, who was her ultimate source. She knew that at this point all she could do was call on God to speak to someone to come to her aid. Happily, a change was on the horizon, because the security guards in the building were tipping her off to which celebrity was going to be on the Steve Harvey show. They even took her PR marketing agency business cards and began to give them to the celebrities that would come through.

One day, Coach Ken Carter, an American businessman, education activist, and high school basketball coach who was portrayed by Samuel L. Jackson in the 2005 movie *Coach Carter*, found her sleeping in her office. He immediately caught on that she must be living there. Initially, she was embarrassed, but it really turned out to be a blessing in disguise. He learned that she was homeless and said, "No women should be living like this."

Her response to him was, "No trust me, I'm okay. I shower at LA Fitness, and I have a routine going on here."

He proceeded to do more digging about her routine and business wins and asked her, "How much money have you made?"

She said "Coach, I made $9,000 last month." As she puts it, she thought she was ballin'. She was saving to get an apartment. He said, "Baby, this is LA. Nine thousand dollars this month is good, but you don't know what you are making the next month, and we don't know how far that is going to go or how long that will last. I'm going to get Paramount to cut you a check." She was very unfamiliar with how that would work, so he went on to explain that the movie studios outsource people to do PR marketing service. He then got her a gig to work on his film.

Once she was aware that movie studios outsource agencies to do their PR, she called William Packer and his business partner Rob Hardy, who are fellow Florida A&M University graduates. Will Packer is known for producing the highly successful movie *Stomp the Yard*, among many other successful movies. She recalled how they would post posters for their DVDs in her boutique. They got her an interview with Sony pictures.

She met with a Sony executive. He loved what she was doing and said she would be a great asset and hired her. She pursued a publicist position for *Stomp the Yard* but was told by the interviewer that she didn't have enough experience. Quick-witted as she was, she told the interviewer that she had a mentor named Rosalind "Roz" Stevenson, the first black executive at Universal and a highly successful film industry publicist. Roz is retired now but is considered a legend in her field. The interviewer knew exactly who Arian was speaking of, and she ended up getting the job.

Roz, however, wasn't Arian's mentor. Arian had only met Roz at an event some time before this interview. She immediately called Roz to let her know that she had dropped her name in the interview and needed her help. Although I don't condone saying someone is your mentor who actually is not, to Arian's advantage, Roz ended up teaching her everything she knew about PR and marketing, including how to do publicity and promotions for a movie. Roz was truly gracious in helping Arian out since she didn't know her, and this situation could have gone the other way. Arian's work was key in helping *Stomp the Yard* become the number one movie two weekends in a row, and at the time it was the third "urban" film, as Arian states, in history to do so. After that, the studio gave her multiple films including *This Christmas* and *First Sunday*. From then on, she received many additional opportunities including the *James Bond* franchise and *Limitless*.

She is now living her dream of helping women of color (WOC) entrepreneurs fund their businesses as a venture capitalist. Her experience with homelessness gave Arian further appreciation for having discipline with money. She didn't want to feel this again or live this way again. Her tenacity and ability to overcome when her challenges seemed insurmountable are inspiring. She began by using and developing the skill sets that were natural to her. Now, she can look back at her many challenges and successes and fully live out her dream of helping WOC just like her fund their start-up companies. Given that women of color entrepreneurs rarely get funding, Arian is creating a platform for that to change. According to an article in *Girlboss*, "Of all VC funding over the past decade, Latinx women-led startups have raised only 0.32 percent while Black women have raised only .0006 percent." Arian is fulfilling her vision from opening her boutique in her college days where she said that one day, she would be the investor she was looking for at that time ("Arian Simone's Fearless Journey" 2012).

Trey Brown: A Teenage Entrepreneur

Meet Trey Brown, the owner of SPERGO. SPERGO is a luxury urban activewear brand. Trey created the brand's name by combining the words "sports," "heroes," and "go"—because SPERGOS are go-getters, as Trey puts it. What's so special about him? Well, he's a successful CEO who started his company on January 15, 2018, at the age of twelve. He started his clothing company out of sheer determination to inspire others to succeed and to create a legacy for himself. I learned so many gems from his *Earn Your Leisure* podcast interview.

Trey has two younger siblings who are being raised by his single mother, Sherell Peterson, a Philadelphia school teacher and creative director of SPERGO. They lived in nine different homes over the course of ten years, in south Philly and northeast Philly, among other neighborhoods. Although he has his mom and family, his address has changed almost every year for most of his childhood. The probability of success when someone doesn't have a stable home is very low. In fact, a *New York Times* article entitled "Does Moving a Child Create Adult Baggage?" shared that "The more times people moved as children, the more likely they were to report lower 'well-being' and 'life satisfaction' as adults (two standard measures used to quantify that ineffable thing called 'happiness')."

However, this is not the case for Trey Brown. He is one who beats all odds. In a video that I watched, posted by the "In the Know" YouTube Channel, I was mesmerized by the confidence in his stride as he walks the streets of Philadelphia metro and ends up on the corner of E Essex Avenue and Wabash Avenue in Lansdowne, Pennsylvania explaining that he made a decision to succeed no matter what. He transparently shares the story of how and why he started SPERGO.

He started SPERGO at a time when there was uncontrollable violence on the streets of Philly. Sadly, there were kids killing kids. He knew there was a better way and wanted to show other kids that there is a better way, too. They can have success without violence or touching any drugs. They can have the jets, the cars, the money without the violence.

Trey has a relentless spirit. He is wise beyond his years. He has this inner drive that comes from somewhere special. He knows the value of community and mentors, too. One day he decided to reach out to Nehemiah Davis, a thirty-one-year-old award-winning author, entrepreneur, and philanthropist born and raised in Philadelphia, who then sent Trey a course on branding and marketing. From that point forward, Nehemiah became Trey's mentor. Nehemiah said about Trey, "He's going to be that kid that's going to be a millionaire, then a billionaire. I believe that wholeheartedly."

After Trey took Nehemiah's courses, he decided to take his birthday money to begin designing T-shirts. He bought and designed his first sixteen T-shirts. He promoted them on Instagram and sold them out in the first week. From there, he began to promote his clothing line to local barber shops. He would spend his Saturdays promoting his business in the streets of Philadelphia door-to-door. He said that most kids his age were doing sports and extracurricular activities on Saturdays. He was out hustling his budding clothing line. He kept selling out and, soon after this repeated success, he built an online business. He sells his clothing all over the world now ("14-Year-Old CEO Retires His Mom" 2020).

After growing his sales and building a significant online platform, Trey garnered the attention of major players in the entertainment industry. He has even appeared on *The Ellen DeGeneres Show* and had the opportunity to finally meet his "mentor in his head," Sean Combs. Sean surprised the young CEO while he was creating an inspiring affirmations commercial for his brand with the help of *The Ellen Show*. Sean Combs presented Trey with a soft black, leather, over-the-shoulder flapover briefcase.

In the video, Trey proceeds to put it over his shoulder and opens it to discover $25,000 worth of cash in the briefcase. Sean says, "I wanna congratulate you, just on your hustle, on making that decision that you was going to make something with your life. ... I don't know how he got my number. He didn't 'regular' call me [for] he would FaceTime me and I was just blown away by his tenacity, by his focus, [and] the quality of his manufacturing. You are a prime example of who we're going to be giving our Black excellence entrepreneur grants to." Both Trey and his mother were elated by this life-changing encounter.

Trey lives and walks his brand. He's consistent. He speaks what he wants to see and will see happen in his life. His daily affirmations consist of these sayings, "I'm powerful. I'm strong. I'm successful. I'm a leader. I'm a winner. I'm a billionaire and I won't stop and I have an impact that is changing the world." At fourteen, he has already "retired" his mother, so yes, he's living up to his SPERGO brand and meaning.

Arian and Trey are wonderful examples of how we can take the challenges we have in life, many that are out of our control, to better our lives and other's lives.

Action Provoking Exercise

- What's one story can you think back on that shows your Tenacity?
- How can you use your Tenacity to help you achieve your financial goals?

CHAPTER 3

NET WORTH

"We don't let the facts get in the way of the truth."
—PASTOR BILL WINSTON

You would think that after five years of getting a good college education and graduating engineering school you'd be all set to properly manage your finances, right? Well, that's not the case. Universities, colleges, and schools in general don't consistently teach financial education.

As I think about why I decided to write this book, I remember when I graduated from The Ohio State University with a BS in electrical and computer engineering. It was June 1998. I was so excited to get a start on life. I was ecstatic to be done with engineering school, as at that point it was the hardest thing I had ever done in my life. I had high hopes for what was ahead of me.

During the first year following graduation, I was introduced to a book called *Rich Dad Poor Dad* by Robert Kiyosaki. It was a life changing book. It's about the father of his good friend (Rich Dad) and Robert's own father (Poor Dad). He compares the two fathers to provide insight into how one becomes prosperous. After reading that book, I had a newfound perspective into my new, fresh-out-of-college job and entrepreneurship. I distinctly remember that I planned to learn as much as I could from my roles at my corporate job and transfer those skills to my own business one day.

I also remember that my father had the book *Think and Grow Rich* by Napoleon Hill. I saw it on his bookshelf in his basement office and I asked him if it was okay for me to borrow and read it. It gave me even more motivation to grow, mature, and achieve greatness. Funny enough, I still have the book and never gave it back. It's a great complement to *Rich Dad Poor Dad*. Both books helped me get into the mindset of wealthy business owners in America. They also challenged me to think about how I may become wealthy and what steps I need to take to grow my net worth.

In August 2000, a few years after I was hired and accepted into the Technical Sales and Marketing Training program at a large manufacturing company. I started working in Philadelphia once I graduated from the program. During my interviews for the Philadelphia role, I was told by my soon-to-be manager that if I could make it in Philly, I could make it anywhere. I decided to take on the challenge of working there. And yes, it was a challenging role for a twenty-five-year-old from the Midwest. The people were tough, and the city was rough. However, I found my tribe of people that I could call friends and developed a community through my church.

When I initially arrived in Philly, I decided to join the Urban League Young Professionals. It was a great way to meet other go-getter young professionals in the city. We would connect and network at the events. We would attend picnics, gala events, and workshops geared toward growing professionally. One event I attended was a financial empowerment fair located in a large room where different company reps manned tables and booths. I stopped by one table, and it was a bank. The young man behind the table was a financial advisor. I was intrigued. I was twenty-five years old, meeting and seeing a financial advisor for the first time.

I remember telling him that I wanted to retire at thirty years old. Thirty was in five years, mind you. He looked at me and didn't say whether I could do it or not, but we decided to meet at his office so that I could start this journey to retiring at thirty. Now, I knew it was lofty, but I believed there was at least a chance. As I began to work with this advisor to set up an account, setting up the account seemed to be the hardest thing ever to do. Unfortunately, he didn't know how to help and in fact may not have known how to do his job as a financial advisor, especially knowing what I know now.

Needless to say, I had to figure everything out on my own. The church that I attended at the time, in Philadelphia, offered a lot of resources on financial literacy. I learned about the importance of credit, of staying debt-free, and about debt elimination. I began to receive some of the foundational information that I had sought from that financial advisor before I knew how to articulate it.

Now I became more curious about the profession. The book *The Purpose Driven Life* was released in 2002, and in that year my friend/roommate from college and I decided to read the book together. It was a life-changing book. As I studied the chapters and began to pray about what in the world I wanted to be when I grew up, I got honest with myself and realized what I was doing at that time—driving around from electrical distributor to electrical distributor and putting on an "act" to sell electrical devices to them—was not what I wanted to do for the next year, let alone the rest of my life. This book helped me realize that.

That year, I made the decision to start a journey toward becoming a financial advisor. I decided that I wanted to help people, especially the youth, build their financial literacy. By around June 2002, I took the Series 7, the Series 66, and the Life and Health Insurance exams and passed. I was on my way to leaving my engineering sales and marketing role and becoming a financial advisor. I knew it was going to be a big jump, but I was excited about the new journey. I knew that I wanted to help people achieve financial success while creating a wonderful path for myself. It was the decision of a lifetime for me at the time.

After a long, challenging, and rewarding journey, I am now at a place where I am working as an entrepreneur. I am a CERTIFIED FINANCIAL PLANNER™ professional, and I'm helping other professionals gain peace of mind and financial security by assisting them with their financial goals.

The State of the Net Worth of Black Families

I have learned over the years that understanding one's net worth is imperative to achieving wealth. Net worth is the most common measure of wealth, determined by taking the total market value of all physical and intangible assets owned, then subtracting all debts (Kelly 2021). According to a Prosperity Now white paper entitled "The Road to Zero Wealth," it will take 228 years for the average Black family to reach the level of wealth white families have today. This white paper also states, "If the racial wealth divide is left unaddressed, median Black household wealth is on the path to hit zero by 2053," whereas the median Latino household wealth is projected to hit zero by 2073, and the median white Household wealth is projected to climb to $137,000 by 2053 and $147,000 by 2073.

When I read this, I was hurt. I was astounded. However, I believe this negative prophecy can be turned around, and I am determined to be part of the solution. According to a Brookings Institution article titled "Closing the racial wealth gap requires heavy, progressive taxation of wealth," "The median white household has a net worth ten times that of the median Black household. According to the 2016 Survey of Consumer Finances, the median white household has a net worth of $171,000, ten times the net worth of the median Black household, $17,100." I share these facts to instill in readers the sense of urgency required to increase one's net worth.

In order to better understand those statistics, let's take a closer look at what assets are. The formal definition of an asset is cash in your checking, savings, and retirement accounts and items such as cars, property, and investments that you could sell for cash, according to a NerdWallet article entitled "Net Worth Calculator: Find Your Net Worth." Examples of assets include real estate, 401(k)s, IRAs, stocks, bonds, mutual funds, savings, cars, and more. The most useful kinds of assets are appreciating and income producing assets. For instance, if one purchases property and rents out the property to cover the mortgage and expenses, with a buffer for income, they are purchasing an income producing asset. The other benefit is that the property has potential to appreciate, meaning it may accumulate value over time. This would be an appreciating asset. In addition, if one purchases a stock, mutual fund, or exchange-traded fund, and it grows, it would be considered an appreciating asset. A stock, bond, mutual fund, or exchange-traded fund that pays dividends is another example of an income producing asset.

On the other hand, a new car is considered a depreciating asset. As soon as you buy a new car it may lose 10 to 15 percent of its value each year, according to the CarsDirect article "Why Does a Car Lose Value After It's Driven off the Lot?" When building your net worth, it's important to make sure you are focused on appreciating and income producing assets. You can easily fall into the "Shiny Object Comparison Trap" and lose sight of the importance of growing your net worth. No one ever compliments us on how our balance sheet looks, but it's more important than that new shiny car everyone sees. You must not lose focus of your vision, values, and goals, which we will discuss throughout the book.

When trying to decide which side of the equation to focus on, understand that if you are reducing your debt, you are increasing your net worth, and if you are increasing your assets, you are increasing your net worth. If you have debt, you need to seriously consider how quickly you can reduce your debt to begin refocusing those debt payments into appreciating and/or income producing assets. This is a life-changing, fundamental equation.

Now that we've discussed the importance of appreciating assets, we will review the definition of liabilities, which means "money you owe to another person or entity" (Bundrick and Ramirez 2020). Let's review some examples of liabilities, which are loans, mortgage, credit cards, student loan debt, car loans, etc. This is the part of the net worth equation that truly affects the net worth of most Americans. According to "The Color of Debt: Credit Card Debt by Race and Ethnicity," a white paper written by an organization called Demos that focuses on research to help grassroots organizations, in 2008, Black Americans had an average $7,390 in debt. The estimated annual percentage rate (APR) paid on credit card debt with the highest balance by Black Americans was 17 percent, which was the highest APR compared to Hispanics and white Americans at 16 percent and 14 percent, respectively. I'm sharing these statistics to help you visualize a better framework for how others are affected by debt. The question is, where do you fall in relation to this debt statistic? Again, it's important to minimize debt, especially consumer debt.

Antoinette Munroe's Story

Antoinette Munroe is an example of a woman who will not allow the statistic to come true for the future of her family legacy. She was born in Miami as the youngest of eight children. She had a happy childhood, never feeling like she lacked anything, and it wasn't until she attended college, Florida A&M University, that she realized she grew up poor.

She never really wanted to work for someone else, but she had incurred $32,000 in debt. She determined that she needed to pay off her debt in two years and then build up $50,000 in savings to live her dream. So she became very diligent about paying off debt and would put $1,000 toward her debt every month. Before long, she had completely paid off her debt.

In order to stay focused on her goals, one activity that Antoinette did was to go to stores like Ross when she was tempted to spend money she didn't want to spend. She would go through the racks and find items that she liked. Then she would fill her cart with those items. Once she got the satisfaction of touching the items, putting them in her basket, and finding other items, she would take the time to put each item back on the rack and leave the store without buying anything unless she absolutely needed it. She called it "therapy." This was her way of achieving the feeling of shopping without compromising her goal of becoming debt-free. She stayed focused and was determined to increase her net worth by decreasing her debt. Once she became debt-free, she started buying property. As of this writing, she owns multiple properties and is building her real estate empire. She eliminated her debt and moved her focus toward increasing her appreciating assets.

From Antoinette's story you see a remarkable example of the importance of building your net worth and understanding it. If you have debt, focus on eliminating debt and focus on increasing your appreciating and income producing assets.

Eric Coleman's Story

Next, let's meet Eric Coleman. At the age of thirty-three, Eric decided that he wanted to retire by forty years old. He was able to achieve that goal and continued to work, by choice, until the age of forty-eight.

Eric Coleman was born in a small town of five hundred people in Kentucky. Growing up in this community helped him see the value of hard work. People got up every day and went to work but didn't really have a concept of building wealth. They were especially unaware of building generational wealth. No one really talked about creating something for the next generation. Eric calls them the working poor, and their main focus was survival.

Ebony, Jet, and *Black Enterprise* magazines were Eric's window to the outside world, showcasing Black success and

Black excellence. He would devour these magazines from cover to cover. However, he realized that most of these successful people were in the entertainment industry working as athletes and actors. He didn't see entrepreneurs until *Black Enterprise* started publishing content featuring entrepreneurs and those amassing great wealth through running successful businesses. This piqued his interests, and he was inspired by the content from *Black Enterprise*, which shares everything from running a business to providing money tips and tools to highlighting those who created impactful companies.

Black Enterprise magazine served as an inspiration for Eric's decision to run his own business one day. He partnered with men from his church in his early twenties. He and his partners started and ran many businesses, from chimney sweeping to lawn care to trucking. They learned many lessons from all the businesses that they started together. He recalls that the chimney sweeping business could have been the most successful business because they had a monopoly in the area for this service. Since they were all afraid of heights, none of them leveraged other services or up-sold opportunities for the chimney sweeping, so they missed out on additional revenue.

Some of the opportunities they missed were being able to provide roofing services and roofing repairs. He recalls that they were probably selling their service too low, and they didn't strategize on how to hire someone who was not afraid of heights to provide that additional business opportunity. They were thinking they had to do everything themselves. By the time they started running the trucking business, they started implementing those valuable lessons such as outsourcing and hiring talent, creating efficient processes, the power of relationships, and how to negotiate large and small contracts. He and his partners ran the trucking business for close to twenty years.

By the time he was thirty-three years old, he began exploring and using other investing strategies outside of his 401(k) by assessing risk management and figuring out how to build his own personal portfolio. He decided that multiple streams of income were imperative. He ended up doing real estate investing, investing in other businesses, creating passive income from stock, freelancing as a business consultant for budding entrepreneurs, and differentiating himself from the competition at his corporate job. He began to use the job as a key component of his wealth building strategy by figuring out how to move through the corporate ranks and building his income from employment.

He also began to strategically utilize the resources he had. Instead of just using his tax preparer to solely prepare taxes, he decided to seek her out for strategies on how to minimize taxes from his job and his business losses. He also hired a financial planner to tell him what he needed to do to retire at fifty years old. By the age of forty, Eric was able to reach his personal definition of financial freedom. Eric says that financial freedom means, "I could go into work at any time. And if I didn't like what I was doing, if I didn't like the way in which I was being treated, or if I just decided I didn't like doing this anymore, that I could walk away from it, and my family would not suffer because I had positioned us to a point where we could still survive without a nine to five job."

Now that's an amazing definition of financial freedom.

His organization, Eric D Coleman Financial Group, is on a mission to create 250,000 millionaires and multi-millionaires. He plans to accomplish this audacious goal over the next ten years and move these households into the top 10 percent of wealth in the United States.

Action Provoking Exercise

- Use your resources and build a team.
    - If you have a tax preparer, find out if they can begin to help you with tax planning strategies instead of just preparing your taxes.
    - Also, utilize a financial planner to help you stay focused on what's important for you to achieve your life financial goals. Maybe you're forty and you want to retire at fifty-five. What needs to be done for you to achieve that goal? How much do you need for income replacement? Where are you now? What is your net worth? How much of your net worth is tied up in liabilities? How much of your net worth is tied up in assets?

- Write out your own personal definition of financial freedom.
- What's your net worth?
    - List all your assets
    - List all your liabilities
    - Net worth = Assets - Liabilities
        - How does your net worth measure up to the averages discussed previously?
        - Are you ahead of the average?
        - Do you have work to do?
        - What are you going to focus on now that you know what your net worth is?

This is a very important exercise because I believe that if you don't know where you are, you most certainly won't know where you are going.

SECTION 2

LIVE
―

Some of us know right away whether we're a saver or a spender. Spenders often get a bad rap, but I believe there is a place for spending. Some examples include spending money as a result of a goal you've achieved, buying a gift for your mother or father, paying for the necessities of life, buying something to improve your health, paying for an estate plan to leave a legacy for your family, and, yes, buying that occasional chai tea latte every now and then. I can go on and on with examples of where spending is good and necessary.

We absolutely cannot go through life without spending money. Spending is part of living. We need to get to a place where we don't feel guilt and shame for spending because we know what our needs are and the purpose of the expense. The reason why spending gets such a bad rap is that it's typically associated with spending too much and spending more than you have. This is what we are working to avoid.

According to Nielsen, the Black community's buying power was $1.4 trillion in 2019 and in 2024 its buying power is projected to be $1.8 trillion. One trillion dollars is a remarkable amount of money. To put it in a way that we can comprehend, the nominal gross domestic product of the United States as a whole is $21.43 trillion (Silver 2020). According to Investopedia, gross domestic product, or GDP, is "the monetary value of all finished goods and services made within a country during a specific period (Fernando 2021).

While Black Americans aren't a country, doing this comparison can give us some frame of reference regarding the spending and buying power of the Black community. The Black community is not too far behind Brazil and Canada, which have a nominal GDP of $1.84 and $1.74 trillion, respectively.

Here's another way to visualize a trillion dollars. According to an article titled "Brain Twister: What does 1 Trillion Look Like?" in *The Dispatch*, "If you had 1 trillion dollar bills, and stacked them up, your tower of money would be about 68,000 miles tall, which would get you about a third of the way to the moon." That is amazing. As you can see, the buying power or spending power of Black communities is pretty notable. For this reason, I want to take the time in this section to review the power of cash flow planning and why it's so important to understand where money is going.

I once heard LeCount Davis, the first Black CERTIFIED FINANCIAL PLANNER™ professional, state something to the effect that if the Black community could take our spending power to increase our investing power, we could be in a better place financially. The Black community has experienced many setbacks and economic injustices, which mustn't go unnoticed. However, it's important for my community to understand that until justice is served, and repairs are made, we must do what we need to do in the meantime. Taking control of our spending is one of the first steps.

CHAPTER 4

THE BETTER RAINY DAYS: SAVINGS AND EMERGENCY FUND

> "Money is only a tool. It will take you wherever you wish, but it will not replace you as the driver."
>
> —AYN RAND

Money is evil. Money is great. Money is everything. Money is bad. Money helps others. Money is a tool. What do you think of when you hear the word money? When we think of money, many perspectives come to mind. Some believe money is the end all be all whereas others believe money is evil.

When we think of money, we need to think of it as a tool. In this chapter, I want to share some key aspects about how money will help you achieve your life's goals. As you explore all the possibilities and create S.M.A.R.T.Y. Goals, you'll quickly realize that very few goals require no money.

Cash Flow Management

One foundational aspect of our money management is your cash flow management. The word budget really makes people nervous, so I am using the term cash flow planning, or cash flow management. I prefer to use budgeting when it comes to making purchases in a few months or over a short period of time.

Cash flow management is another aspect of financial wellness and taking control of your money. I believe it's probably the foundation of your financial wellness. It's extremely important to track your income and expenses, and tools for tracking will make your life so much easier. You may use ones such as YNAB.com, Excel, pen and paper, MINT, Tiller, or whatever you prefer. With these types of tools, you will have the ability to see visually how you're spending your money. It's important to find what tool works best. Get as deep and detailed as you want.

First, take the time to look at where you can decrease expenses. Can you cut back on your coffee runs and make coffee at home? Are you using that gym subscription? Do you really need cable? What about replacing cable with Netflix, Sling, or YouTube TV? What alternatives are out there to replace what you are spending money on? Can you replace watching TV with reading a book in your library? Can you go to the public library to check out the media offered? Are you spending too much money dining out? Maybe get creative in the kitchen and develop a wonderful at-home dining experience.

All my life, I have been a fan of cooking shows. I would say watching cooking shows is truly a pastime for me. I enjoy cooking but only when the conditions are right, and my obligations are light. However, since the start of the pandemic of 2020, with nowhere else to go, I ended up having no choice but to cook from home. I also decided to make a dietary change, so I wasn't eating all the meals restaurants offered anyway. I started to put all my cooking knowledge to use and began making some really tasty creations. It actually became fun and, by not eating out as frequently, I saved money.

If you aren't using your gym membership or you're willing to cancel your gym membership to save money, then hike outside instead of going to the gym. You can even do a search on YouTube for pretty much any type of workout you are interested in. There are so many free resources on what I call "YouTube University." I, by no means want to rain on your "fun" parade, but sometimes we have to practice discipline and patience in order to reach our goals.

In my practice I have my clients use a tool called Winton, which was developed by Stephanie Holmes-Winton, founder of CacheFlo, Inc. It allows people to categorize their expenses into "committed expenses" and "spendable expenses." Committed expenses are those that don't have emotional risk and fluctuate only slightly if at all. Committed expenses include your rent/mortgage, utilities, cable bill, internet bill, savings, etc. Spendable expenses are those expenses that fluctuate regularly due to emotions and therefore have emotional risk. Your spendable expenses are those expenses that vary from month to month like gifts, groceries, dining out, etc. Using groceries in the spendable expenses category is more accurate than putting them on the committed expense side, since you can go to a grocery store on any given day to buy milk, apples, contact lens solution, a dress, and a patio set. Case in point: even if I have a grocery store list for fruit and vegetables, I'll find myself buying another fruit that I didn't think of until I see it at the store. Your grocery store purchases are susceptible to emotional spending.

As a best practice to have more control over your spending, you will want to create a few bank accounts. At a minimum you need two separate bank accounts: one main account holding your committed expenses and another bank account for your spendable expenses. All your income sources will feed into the committed expenses bank account. From the committed account you will want to transfer money needed for your spendable expenses to your spendable account. It's also a great idea to have additional accounts connected to your committed expense account to hold your emergency savings, and it's best to make it difficult to get to your emergency savings so that you have it when you need it and aren't tempted to use it for frivolous spending.

Take advantage of automating your savings as well. I'm a believer in creating a path of least resistance, thus reducing friction. If you don't have to think about how much to save or when to save, then you will have a higher chance of success. Most bank accounts allow you to make recurring deposits in or out of accounts. Once you determine how much you need for your committed expenses and how much you need for spendable expenses, set this up and monitor it so that you make sure it's working properly and doing what you want. It's important to transfer money from your committed expenses account to your spendable account on a weekly basis. For example, if you determine that you need $1,000 per month for spendable expenses that means you will divvy out $250 per week instead of transferring $1,000 all at once. You want to spread it out on a weekly basis so that you don't spend your $1,000 before the month is over. Statistically, when you divide your funds on a monthly basis, the money only lasts 18.25 days. If you find yourself not having enough money to last the whole month, this could be a reason why. Creating a system for where your money is going will help you get a handle on it without the need to do line by line accounting.

Multiple Income Sources

Another opportunity for financial wellness is to increase your income sources. One of the things I keep hearing is that we need to have anywhere from seven to eight streams of income. I am a believer in multiple streams of income. Just like an emergency fund will help us handle the unexpected, having multiple streams of income will also help us when unexpected financial changes occur.

I was convinced by this concept after attending a workshop at my church in Orlando conducted by Robert J. Watkins who is an international financial and business trainer. He taught the attendees that we should begin to build our income streams. Many of us are indoctrinated into getting a good job with benefits and that's it. And typically, it's not until we get married that we have more than one income. I am now convinced that it's detrimental to not have more than one stream of income whether you are single or married. In addition to having an emergency fund, at least one additional stream of income is life-changing for your financial wellness.

Tom Corley, author of an article entitled "Create Wealth Like the Rich with Multiple Streams of Income," said he "learned that most self-made millionaires generated their income from multiple sources and sixty-five percent had three streams of income, forty-five percent had four streams of income, twenty-nine percent had five or more streams of income." However, we can only go so far when it comes to utilizing trading time for money in creating additional streams of income. Some ideas for additional income streams include creating an online shop to sell T-shirts, investing, starting an online business, creating online courses, etc.

When I say this, folks get a bit overwhelmed. If you're feeling overwhelmed, start with your present employment. That is one stream of income. Then ask yourself if you are an essential worker. With the COVID-19 pandemic, I realized how important it is to recession proof your income. If your occupation is not considered essential, what other income streams can you start to pursue and grow? List your skill sets and match them up to jobs or businesses that still thrive in times of economic stagnancy.

The Power of Pivot, Reframing and Staying Relevant

Keba Konte is one such person who was able to create and maximize what was at his fingertips to create more cash flow so that his business would survive during the pandemic and beyond.

Keba's story is a testament to the fact that we can have multiple talents and marry them with a vision. He is a visual artist in the areas of photojournalism, music photography, and visual fine arts. He is the owner of an innovative coffee company called Red Bay Coffee Roasters, which is located in the San Francisco Bay Area. It was founded in 2014 and seeks to create a unified and diverse environment for people of all backgrounds who have traditionally been left out of the specialty coffee industry, especially people of color, the formerly incarcerated, women, and people with disabilities. He doesn't equate his success in the specialty coffee business to his coffee roasting skills or his cappuccino and latte art skills, but his success is in his "… ability to create an environment, create a concept that inspires people and that a lot of people want to be down with."

Before opening his coffee shop, Keba earned what he calls a very general speech communications degree in college. He had no idea what he'd do with it but realizes that everything he's done has led him to where he is today. He is a renowned artist. He is a storyteller. He uses photojournalism and what he calls individual storytelling to share compelling stories and inspiration. All these talents and experiences led Keba to becoming an owner of a coffee shop.

Keba never thought that he'd be an owner of a coffee shop. He originally got into coffee to further his art career. When offered the opportunity to open a café in North Berkeley, he thought it would be a great opportunity to showcase his artwork. As he reflects on where he started, he realizes it's something that he's been ironically preparing for his whole life. His entrepreneurial lifestyle running a successful art photography business and showing up for his community through community activism initiatives aided him in attracting this opportunity in the first place. When this opportunity came his way, he became fascinated and captivated with working in the hospitality industry, manufacturing and working directly with farmers.

Keba says one of the best decisions he ever made was marrying his wife, Rachel (pronounced Raquel), who is a key part of his ability to take advantage of the opportunity he was given to buy his first coffee shop. At the time, his wife had a corporate job in design and, with their combined interests and income, the two of them were able to buy the shop. He points out how important it is that he and his wife are supportive of each other as they pursue these entrepreneurial goals. I would agree. If one has a spouse, their support is imperative to success.

Keba shares that he has to convince his wife every day in many of his endeavors, but it's more about how they complement each other. They each bring different strengths to the relationship: his wife is more of the rational designer who takes a more cautious and deliberate approach to decision-making, whereas he is the guerilla artist political activist who is the dreamer or inspirationalist. The two perspectives of their personalities bring more harmony to their relationship. He said if it wasn't for his wife's counterbalance, this whole thing (his business) would have spun out of control and burned out a long time ago.

One thing that is for sure about entrepreneurship and business is that there will be ups and downs. Keba, like many entrepreneurs of 2020 had to pivot, reframe, and stay relevant due to the impact of COVID-19. Red Bay Coffee Roasters saw its revenue plummet by 90 percent in a short period of time. Prior to March 2020, 60 percent of Red Bay's revenue came from tech companies such as Facebook, Airbnb, Twitter, Square, and many similar companies. Another 30 percent of its revenue was generated from its five different coffee shops. Its coffee shop also served as a venue for concerts, weddings, corporate meetings, film festivals, etc., which was revenue lost due to COVID-19.

When COVID-19 hit, only essential businesses could remain open. At that moment, there was not a real definition of essential, however. It was a confusing time, and while the company was trying to determine if its business was considered essential or not, its revenue dropped by 90 percent in a matter of a couple of days. To rectify this situation, first Keba had to turn off all its spending, which painfully included furloughing some of his employees. The operation moved from having sixty employees to six employees. He had to cut Wi-Fi in coffee shops. He had to stop paying insurance, rent, and any bill that didn't need his immediate attention.

Then the company reached out to its community to let them know what was happening. From there, the community began to purchase coffee from Red Bay's e-commerce platform. At the time, e-commerce was such a small part of its business that it wasn't even a part of its revenue projections. Fortunately, the company had invested in the infrastructure as something that it would do one day but the pandemic accelerated the need for the company to pivot to e-commerce much sooner than it imagined.

After about a week from closing all Red Bay's shops, he, his wife, and his daughter decided to reopen one of the shops. Because they bought bulk orders of milk (conventional and plant-based) and other staples, they were able to reframe the store as an essential business by selling those grocery items directly to customers.

As for coffee consumption, they realized that people weren't drinking any less coffee but that their consumption patterns had changed, and they had to change with it. They even got some traction with the tech companies whose employees were now working from home, by providing coffee as an "at-home" perk to their work from home employees. A few weeks later they reopened another shop. Some employees came back, and some didn't due to the risks associated with

COVID-19 and how it might impact their families. There were lots of changes to endure.

After a few more months, they realized that it was going to take longer to get "back to normal," which meant some of those furloughs turned into layoffs. This was extremely difficult for Keba because those employees were great people, and they were doing their jobs well. Keba and his team had to make many hard decisions during this time. They came to grips with the fact that things that were "nice to have" before, like the Wi-Fi, were truly optional at this point. They were trying to make sure that the bare necessities were taken care of.

Prior to the pandemic, Keba was already working on an initiative to have a mobile coffee vehicle. During the early chaos of 2020, it just so happened that the Mercedes Sprinter van he had planned to use for mobile coffee was ready. However, they didn't have a city permit. Fortunately, the cities and the counties weren't enforcing regulations, as they understood the times of survival. The van would sell coffee in the Lake Merritt area. However, that soon came to an end when more businesses caught wind of it, and it began to draw more crowds. Due to concerns about spreading COVID-19, the city decided to shut the whole lake down as a safety measure.

In late May 2020 came the murder of George Floyd, which reignited the Black Lives Matter movement and initiated a campaign to support Black-owned businesses. That pushed their e-commerce platform even further and, by June, Red Bay Coffee was doing $250,000 in sales in e-commerce only. Their e-commerce platform wasn't built for that much volume, but the team continued to tweak it and improve their site. Then it was featured in the *Forbes* article "100 Black-Owned Businesses to Support," which helped it gain more momentum. That article led me to reach out to Keba.

Next, the company made an *O Magazine* list entitled "25 Black-Owned Businesses You Can Support Right Now," which boosted growth. Then, during the Christmas season, Red Bay Coffee was listed as Oprah's favorite coffee on Oprah's favorite things list. With that major boost, it was able to partner with Amazon and hire a digital marketer to ensure it could meet the demand of its online sales. In addition, due to the moves the team was making and how they were staying relevant to the times and growing their business, they were able to secure a bridge loan from their investors to make all of this happen. They are even developing a canned coffee beverage to allow for single use coffee service to minimize human interactions due to the pandemic.

The Red Bay Coffee story is still unfolding, but they were able to take the challenges and unexpected setbacks and turn them into triumphs. Keba decided that stories such as his are relevant to other founders, so he decided to launch a podcast to continue to tell these stories. The new podcast is called *Coffee Dojo*. It's amazing to hear stories such as these because many will see the glitz and the glamour and rest on that. However, there's so much more to know behind the scenes about the stories of triumph and overcoming. Keba and his team had to make major adjustments and many difficult decisions to stay afloat and stay around for the people they serve.

When it comes to personal finances, whether one is an entrepreneur or intrapreneur, there are moments when one must decide what is absolutely important to reaching one's financial goals. We must realize that there is an ebb and flow to this personal finance journey, that we will have times of survival, times of maintenance, and times of growth. It can be risky, and there are no right or wrong answers when one is in the thick of it. I am reminded in this story that Keba and his company had to reach out to the community to let them know that they were in trouble. From there, they were able to secure the help they needed. Even with personal finance, there is a point where you need to reach out to the community to find resources such as books, podcasts, tools, a friend, a program, and/or a financial planner to help you create a game plan to get out of a slump. We are not alone, and it's important to hear these stories.

Preparing for the Unexpected: Emergency Funds

The next item to consider is your emergency funds. It's so important to have emergency fund money because you can't predict when you'll need it. Because life is full of the unexpected, it is not if something will happen but when something will happen.

In 2020, due to the CARES Act, many people were provided with a stimulus check, and for a lot of people, the stimulus check amount did not cover much. But it may have covered all or part of one month's rent. The stimulus check is a windfall of money. A windfall is money that comes unexpectedly. If you're out of debt, then I recommend you put it toward your three- to six-month emergency fund.

When determining how much of an emergency fund is needed, it's best to figure out what your essential needs are. I recommend looking at your housing, food, and transportation needs. Those are the bare essentials. Determine what they cost and multiply it by three to get three months, and six to get six months. For example, if you need $1,200 per month for rent/mortgage, $400 per month for food, and $500 for transportation, then you will need $6,300 for three months and $12,600 for six months.

If you have multiple streams of income, you may not need as many months saved up. Assess that yourself. For example, if you have two income streams coming into your household, whether it's a husband-and-wife situation and you're both working or if you're single person with more than one income stream, you may not need as many months for an emergency fund because you have another income source to fall back on.

Three to six months is a good rule of thumb for your essential expenses. Essential expenses that will most likely fall into the Committed Expenses category previously discussed include shelter, utilities, and transportation. You can dine out if you feel that you're never going to cook but find ways to lower expenses elsewhere if you're in an emergency situation. Essential expenses do not include the cable box. The key to financial wellness is to determine what is important and make sure it aligns with your values so you can reach your goals. Always remember: the sacrifice will be worth it for the reward and peace of mind.

Action Provoking Exercise

- What are your committed expenses?
- What are your spendable expenses?
- Do you have a deficit or a surplus?
- If you have a surplus, how can you allocate those funds toward a goal?
- If you have a deficit, where do you need to lower your expenses?
- What other income streams can you start to pursue and grow?
- List your skill sets and match them up to jobs or businesses that still thrive in times of economic stagnancy.
- Is there an online business you can start?
- Can you teach something online and monetize it?
- How much do you need for an emergency fund?
- Do you need to save more or is your emergency fund full?

CHAPTER 5

PROTECT YOUR WEALTH: ARE YOU ON TEAM "BOUNCE MY LAST CHECK?"

"One of the most caring things you can do is to prepare for your death so that the living can have peace of mind is to have an estate plan."

When I first started out as a financial advisor, I met with a woman in her sixties who seemed to be doing well financially. When I asked her how she planned to provide for her heirs, she immediately responded, "I'm going to bounce my last check just like my father did." Her father was her example. She said he lived a great life, he saved money for his retirement, and he was able to do the things he wanted to do to provide for himself. She admired that about him, and she also admired that he had no money left over for anyone when he passed away.

Now, that was the first time I ever heard anyone use that phrase, "Bounce my last check." From that point forward, I never forgot that statement. When it comes to leaving a financial legacy for heirs, there are people who are on team "bounce my last check" or team "leave money for generations to come." This chapter is for those who are on the latter team. I'm of the mindset that "a good man leaves an inheritance to his children's children" (Proverbs 13:22 NKJV).

Given that Black wealth is projected to decline to zero by 2053. I believe it's my responsibility to discuss the importance of passing on wealth to the next generation. "Individuals that start life with little or no wealth are often trapped at the bottom of the wealth distribution for their entire lives. More than half of white families end up with more wealth than their parents, while only 23 percent of Blacks are able to do the same," according to an article written by Janelle Jones called "Receiving an Inheritance Helps White Families More Than Black Families."

When I talk about protecting your wealth, I like to compare it to a castle and a fortress. The other topics that I discussed are like the chambers in your castle, such as cash flow planning, investing, setting goals, exploring possibilities, retirement planning, etc. However, what good is it to accumulate your wealth but have no protection for it should you pass away or something unexpected happens? Castles are protected either by a big wall or a moat or both to make sure that the enemy cannot easily gain access to the castle. Likewise, it's important to protect your assets. Protecting your wealth can help to alleviate fear, anxiety, and loss.

The most basic way to protect is to have an emergency fund. As stated in the previous chapter, an emergency fund is designed to protect you from unforeseen circumstances such as the AC going out in your car or your house, your roof needing repairing, or even an unexpected layoff at your job. The emergency fund is one way to create peace of mind so that you know you have a plan should the worst situation happen. I often say we are not predicting that the bad situation will occur, but we want to make sure that we have the best situation should the worst happen. It is recommended to have at least three to six months of an emergency fund. If one is retired, I recommend at least a twelve-month emergency fund.

Disability Insurance

Another way to protect your fortress is preparing for your income replacement should you become injured and cannot work any longer. The likelihood of becoming disabled is very high for young professionals. In fact, the Social Security Administration states in an article entitled, "The Faces and Facts of Disability," that for "twenty-year-olds… more than 1-in-4 of them becomes disabled before reaching retirement age." This is quite sobering since this is the last thing twenty-year-olds are thinking about. Should you become disabled, you have to think about how you are going to continue to meet your financial obligations. You also have to think about the values that you have. Loss of income impedes one's ability to make a living and to be independent. If independence is an important value for you, which I'm sure it is, then you absolutely need to make sure you have a plan in place. The solution is to have disability insurance.

Disability insurance helps you in case you have lost income. The duration of the average long-term disability is 34.6 months. According to the Council for Disability

Awareness, most Americans do not have this. Disability insurance is a way to protect your income should you become injured and can no longer perform the duties of your work. There are different types of disability insurance to consider, but the main ones to consider are own-occupation, any-occupation or a combination of own-occupation and any-occupation. Understanding these definitions is very important because they explain how you get paid should an injury occur.

If you purchase an any-occupation long-term disability insurance policy, it means that if you are able to work any type of job, even if it's lower paying, your long-term disability, benefits will not kick in. On the other hand, there's a type of policy called the own-occupation policy, which means that if you are unable to perform your own-occupation for which you are trained, your long-term disability income benefits will be paid, even if you are able to work. The own-occupation type policy is far superior to any-occupation, but it is also more expensive. It's important to understand what type of policy you have as it can make a world of difference in how you plan your future.

Life Insurance

Another way to protect your wealth is to have life insurance. The name life insurance can seem a bit misleading as it only pays out to the beneficiaries after the insured passes away. However, the importance of life insurance can be a game changer. When I used to live in Phoenix, Arizona it saddened me to see the families on the street corners hosting car washes to pay for the death of their loved ones. In today's age, we may not see as many families doing car washes, but we see them hosting community funding campaigns through crowdfunding sites. It's not bad to do this, but many are doing it from a lack of planning. Life insurance could have prevented that.

Life insurance is a game changer when it comes to creating generational wealth. However, Black Americans have a tarnished history with life insurance. From the history in the United States, companies like New York Life would offer life insurance to enslavers if the enslaved human that they owned died. It was utterly atrocious to conceive, but New York Life offered death benefits to the enslavers for three quarters of the value of this human's life. Of course, the value of a human life is priceless, but during these times an evaluation was done. These types of life insurance policies accounted for about one third of the policies for the company (Swarns 2016). Other companies that insured the lives of enslaved Africans were Aetna and US Life, just to name a few.

The Black community has a complicated relationship with life insurance. For a long time, many Black Americans associated life insurance with covering burial expenses and didn't look at it from a wealth-building-vehicle perspective. Burial expense policies are small and only cover burial, not passing on wealth to the next generation. Also, the policies offered very high premiums compared to the benefits pay out. "These practices led to litigation and settlements that were resolved not that long ago," says Judy Hopkins, head of legal at Haven Life (Eagan 2020).

I remember my mother telling me my grandad purchased life insurance for all his grandchildren. He was told that it was a way to pass on wealth to the next generation. When my beloved granddad passed away, my mother remembered the certificates that grandad purchased. She soon discovered they were no longer valid, and the policies were not in force any longer. From what we know, the premiums became too high for my grandfather to afford. I can only assume how upset my grandfather felt at having put money into those policies for the benefit of his grandchildren only to have nothing to show for them in the end. It makes me wish I knew more about what he had purchased and why the premium went up so high. It's really sad, but these are examples as to why Black Americans are distrustful of insurance.

Another note is that after the Civil War, life insurance policy insurers classified former enslaved Africans as having a higher mortality risk than their white counterparts, so the policies were overly expensive. These practices continued. "Some states banned race-based underwriting, but many insurers simply took their business elsewhere, reducing access to coverage and segregating the industry" (Rose 2021).

Due to these many factors and the complicated relationship between life insurance and the Black community, Black Americans are more likely to see the value of purchasing life insurance as a means to pass on wealth to the next generation than white Americans. "A new survey from Haven Life shows that twenty-two percent of Blacks value life insurance as a way to pass along generational wealth compared to only eight percent of white respondents (Egan 2020)." Although Black Americans believe life insurance is a way to pass on wealth, many Black Americans don't have enough coverage. According to the Haven Life Insurance survey, "The median income for Black survey takers was $50,162 and $54,823 for white survey takers. However, white respondents had a median coverage of $150,000, while Black respondents reported having just $50,000 in coverage" (Medine 2020).

A good rule of thumb in determining how much coverage is needed is six to twelve times your income. Unfortunately, both groups are underinsured in this case, but life insurance is actually not very expensive. Now, there are two main types of life insurance: term insurance and permanent insurance. Term insurance costs less because it insures for a certain period of time, whereas permanent insurance is for the rest of one's life. Term insurance helps to alleviate that cost barrier. Black Americans perceive life insurance to be higher than it really is. However, it's not that expensive at all. For example, "a healthy thirty-four-year-old woman can buy a twenty-year, $250,000 term life insurance policy for as little as sixteen dollars per month," according to the article entitled "Is there a life insurance race gap?" According to Haven Life, "a thirty-five year old man who's in excellent health and a non-smoker would pay around twenty-three dollars a month for a twenty year, $500,000 policy. At age forty-five, that man would pay about fifty-six dollars a month for the same coverage." (Egan 2020) The best way to think about life insurance is that if your income is meant to take care of other family members how would they survive financially if you were to pass away? That is the question that needs to be answered when determining how much coverage is needed. Once you see how much is needed, you must take action by purchasing a life insurance policy, and that would be done with a trusted financial planner or life insurance agent.

Estate Planning

I need to preface this section with the fact that I am not an attorney and therefore do not provide legal advice. This section will serve as guidance for what you need to do to prepare for your legacy.

Estate planning is the most caring thing you can do for your family. It's difficult to discuss what will happen to us and our belongings when we pass away, but again, we are not predicting that the worst will happen—we're planning for the best situation should the worst happen. The time it takes to get everything set up is going to be worth it. When I ask people what having a financial plan will do for them, many answer that it will give them peace of mind. Having an estate plan is one of the keys to peace of mind. A common misconception with estate planning is that it's only for the wealthy. This is not true—one thing I can guarantee is that we are all going to die, so if you have loved ones and you want to create a legacy, you don't have to be wealthy to make sure your loved ones receive your possessions.

You designate a beneficiary as well. Naming a beneficiary means to select a person that you want to give money should you pass away. According to an article entitled "Over half of Americans saving for retirement make a money mistake you can fix in just three minutes," 60 percent of Americans haven't named a beneficiary on their retirement accounts (Jackson 2019). It doesn't take long to do this task, but many forget this step. I know a lot of people want to create generational wealth. Adding a beneficiary to your retirement accounts and insurance accounts is a quick and easy first step to creating a legacy. This goes for every account that you have, as a matter of fact. It's a good practice to ensure that beneficiaries are named on your IRAs, retirement plans at work such as 401(k)s, TSPs, 403(b)s, 457 plans, and Roth IRAs, and any account that allows you to add a beneficiary. What if you were divorced and you passed away and the beneficiaries were never updated before your passing? Your ex-spouse would get the funds that you intended for your new spouse or children or other important family members to receive. Another reason to have named beneficiaries is that accounts that don't have beneficiaries listed go through the probate process. The probate process is the process that your possessions go through after you die to distribute to the heirs. When you set up a will, you will go through probate. The probate process is a public process. If you are a private person, having all your possessions listed for the world to see is not fun. The process of setting up your beneficiaries is really quick and easy, so it's important to take the time to perform this task.

A will is a way to protect your assets. A will allows you to express your wishes regarding how you'd like your possessions distributed. It helps to alleviate your heirs from "spending additional time, money and emotional energy to settle your affairs after you're gone" (Smith 2021). A will can alleviate family misunderstandings and promote unity in the family, especially during such a difficult time as a loved one's death. Furthermore, if you have children, a will spells out who will take care of them should you pass away instead of the courts deciding. Although you can access plenty of resources online, it's best to hire an estate planning attorney to prepare your will or trust.

Another way to protect your assets is to set up a trust. A trust is more expensive upfront but it's private, meaning that it doesn't go into public record. A will goes into public record. The formal definition of a trust as defined by Investopedia is: "Trusts are established to provide legal protection for the trustor's assets, to make sure those assets are distributed according to the wishes of the trustor, and to save time, reduce paperwork and, in some cases, avoid or reduce inheritance or estate taxes (Kagan 2020)." Basically, a trust is a way for you to protect your assets. Once a trust is created, it's important to retitle assets in the name of the trust. That way you know you have the protection desired, and the assets will go to the appropriate person.

Trusts are important because they can make life simpler. I remember having a client who received an inheritance from an aunt. Unfortunately, the aunt didn't have beneficiaries named. She had a will, but it was out of date. The niece had to start the probate process and even though she knew that her aunt wanted her to have the possessions as she was the next of kin, the probate process made it public and allowed for any other creditors or relatives to contest and try to get her aunt's possessions. Fortunately, no one else laid claim to the assets, but the fact that there were no beneficiaries on the IRA or other assets made the legal process long and drawn out—all of which could have been avoided. I watched how stressed the client was going through this process. She even mentioned that not only does having the will, trust, or beneficiaries alleviate stress for the heirs, but the heirs have to go through the deceased's possessions and make decisions on everything. If the deceased didn't spell out their wishes beforehand, then a lot of burden is placed on the heir(s), which is difficult when you are mourning the loss of your loved one. The client was certainly grateful for receiving the assets, but it was an emotionally taxing position to be in. It's hard to think about the fact that we'll die one day but for those left behind, we should take the time to make the process as stress free as possible.

There are some additional documents that you must have that are important regarding estate planning. A power of attorney (POA) "is a legal document in which the principal (you) designates another person to act on your behalf" (Rotter

2021). You may get a durable POA, which lasts a lifetime, or a springing POA, which usually activates due to incapacity. A medical power of attorney is a legal document that appoints an agent to make health care decisions on behalf of a principal who is unable to make those decision for themselves. An advanced medical directive aka a living will is a legal document expressing an individual's last wishes regarding the sustainment of their life under specific circumstances. You should also consider the do-not-resuscitate order, or DNR, which declares the principal's wish to avoid having CPR performed in the event their heart stops beating. The act of taking the time to take care of this is going to go back to your values. It's so important and, again, one of the most loving acts that you can do for your family and loved ones.

Another thing to do is to make sure that your heirs know how to access to all of your computer systems and any system that requires a password. Can you imagine your loved one passing away and you having no way to access any of their information? It's important to have a conversation with someone you trust to make sure they can get into your systems. There are many password management systems to utilize so that you may provide access to your family members or someone you trust should they need access to important documents and information. You may even consider creating a "love letter" or writing something that puts context to your wishes that make it more personal.

Action Provoking Exercise

- What values most align with why you will get an estate plan taken care of?
- Do you have an estate plan?
- Do you have a health care directive?
- Living will?
- Do you need a trust or a will?

SECTION 3

SAVE

By the end of 2018, the total debt of all Americans stood at $13.5 trillion (Nieves 2019). At that time, there were about 126 million households, which means that if we average the total debt amongst all the households, it would equate to $135,000 of debt per household. The numbers are astounding. According to Prosperity Now's report called "Overdue: Addressing Debt in Black Communities" by Pamela Chan et al., the debt of Black households is at $30,800, and the debt of white families is at $73,800. Even with Black families' debt being lower, over 25 percent of Black families report being late with debt payment companies compared to 15 percent of White families.

Although Black families reportedly have less debt than White families, Black households have more trouble making payments due to the "legacy of discrimination" that has left Black Americans with few assets. Unfortunately, Black Americans on average tend to make less than white Americans so they are unable to make the payments as readily. Black Americans will likely not have the fortune to tap into assets like savings and homes to make debt payments if all their resources are exhausted. It's troubling.

As a financial planner, I want people to understand these facts and challenges and determine to not be one of these horrible statistics. Now, more than ever, it's important to minimize what one owes and begin to save. The sacrifices necessary to make this happen will be deeply personal. However, it's important to note that it's not impossible and that everyone can have their own timeframe to achieve debt freedom. The sooner you are out of debt, the sooner you can save. The sooner you are out of the debt, the sooner you can experience stress relief. The sooner you are out of debt, the sooner you can experience peace of mind that your family will be taken care of.

There are so many benefits to experiencing and achieving debt freedom on the road to financial freedom. What will life be like for you once you experience debt freedom?

I believe some will answer that once they are debt-free they will be able to save more. This is exciting. Savings in the bank can make you feel more secure. This feeling of security can help you see possibilities and even dream again. How much savings do you want? How much savings do you need? In this section, we'll focus on the importance of relating savings to short-term goals, mid-term goals, and long-term goals. I plan to discuss my money buckets strategy and why it's important to know your savings goals and the time frame that coincides with those goals.

CHAPTER 6

DON'T PUT ALL YOUR MONEY IN ONE BUCKET

"When the purpose of a thing is not known, abuse is inevitable."

—MYLES MUNROE

When I first heard this quote by the late Dr. Myles Munroe, it truly resonated with me. Soon after college, when I first started my job, I saved as much as I could into my 401(k) at work. It was the only thing I really knew to do at the time. However, as I got older, I realized I didn't have a down payment to buy a house or an emergency fund for unexpected expenses. Fortunately, I learned about this before I really needed it, but it's really telling that I hadn't learned about these concepts with all the education I had up to that point.

Once I realized that withdrawing from my 401(k) to take care of a big expense or an emergency before 59.5 years old would cause me to pay income tax plus a ten percent penalty,

I knew I had to create a strategy. Over the years, I started teaching about how I compartmentalize money. I found that some of my clients would complain about their 401(k) because when they wanted to withdraw, they learned how difficult and expensive it is.

I believe it's important to split our money into buckets, so I decided to create an understandable way to compartmentalize your money.

The Short-Term Money Bucket

The first bucket is for short-term goals. I define short-term goals as goals that are five years or less. These goals would include saving for an emergency or saving for any goal that you would like to accomplish in a short period of time. Funding vehicles for this type of goal would be a savings account, checking account, money market account, or even a certificate of deposit. You want to make sure that your money is liquid for your short-term goals. It would be terrible if you placed your money into a high-risk stock or mutual fund for a short-term goal, and right when you need the money, the market takes a major downturn. However, at this point, you take the money because you're using it to fund an emergency. This is what we are trying to avoid with this strategy. We also create accounts for your short-term savings so you can avoid having to go into debt. Remember: it's not if an emergency happens, but when it happens. We want to prepare for the best situation should the worst happen. Take a moment to review the chapter where I discuss the "Emergency Fund."

The Mid-Term Money Bucket

The next bucket of the three money buckets is the one that I think gets missed most frequently. The two goals we hear the most are emergency funds and retirement funds. We rarely hear about the mid-term bucket. I actually think I should call this the "fun bucket" because this is the bucket that I associate with those goals that allow you to live the life you've imagined. The mid-term bucket is for goals you want to accomplish in the next five to fifteen years. The goals in this bucket are associated with taking a dream vacation, buying something you really want, a down payment on a first home or second home on the beach, a major gift you want to buy for your mom's milestone birthday, etc. This is the bucket where you can really dream about what you want and develop a strategy toward reaching those goals.

The types of vehicles you would use to fund this type of goal could be any of the vehicles mentioned in the short-term money bucket, as well as investment type accounts, like a brokerage account that holds mutual funds, stocks, and exchange-traded funds. You can take more risk depending on your risk tolerance because you will have the ability to withstand the ups and downs of the market over time. Again, having a proper discussion with your financial planner would be beneficial in making sure you find the right investment that fits your risk profile.

The Long-Term Money Bucket

The third money bucket is the long-term money bucket. This bucket is for your long-term goals. Long-term goals are goals that will take you fifteen plus years to complete. Great examples of long-term goals are retirement, passing on money to heirs, paying off a house, and many more. Once you determine your long-term goals, you can give yourself the opportunity to let your money work harder for you by investing. Vehicles that are suitable for long-term goals such as retirement would be a 401(k), IRA, Roth IRA, TSP, etc. These are vehicles that allow for tax deferral, which means that you don't have to pay taxes on the money until you withdraw it. If you're under 59.5 years old then there's income tax plus a 10 percent penalty, and if you're over 59.5 you can withdraw the funds and not pay a penalty but, depending on the type of account, you will have to pay income tax. You will need to consult your tax advisor for further details pertaining to your situation.

Investment Accounts

Let's talk a little more about investment accounts. A retirement account is a type of investment account. However, you can and should have investment accounts outside of retirement. I believe those accounts need to be aligned with your goals. Perhaps you have a goal that you want to buy a car in ten years, or you want to take your family on a trip five years from now. Instead of just putting it into a regular savings account, you can look at an investment account. An investment account is an opportunity to have your money working a little bit harder for you.

Your emergency fund would be more of a low-yield, low-risk account. The investment account, on the other hand, is going to be in something a little bit riskier than your regular savings. With that being said, we're going to talk about risk tolerance because it's important to understand that fluctuations are inevitable with investing. You should understand how much fluctuation you can handle.

When you work with a financial planner like me, they will have a conversation with you about your risk tolerance and have you take an assessment. They will determine your capacity and how you respond when the market goes down. Are you the type of person who will email or call your financial advisor to say, "Hey! We've got to pull out of this!"? Are you going to be the person that calls and says, "You know what, I want to buy some more"? Knowing your response is key when determining your risk tolerance.

Also keep in mind your time horizon. A time horizon is how long you want to have the funds invested. A great way to determine that is to decide if it's a long-term, short-term, or mid-term goal. Everybody has a different time frame depending on their goal.

Your time horizon is going to determine how much risk you need to take as well. For example, let's say you invested money in January of a particular year, and you told me that you wanted it to be around for the long term. Then I'm probably going to put you in something that is going to take on a little more risk so that you can get a little bit more reward. However, if you call me in March because the market went down and you're ready to withdraw all those funds, then we need to have another talk. At that point, you're going to lose money. We don't want to do that. Thus, knowing your time horizon for the money that you're investing is imperative. Note: investing for the long term doesn't guarantee against loss.

There's also the Rule of 72. I like this rule because it gives you a vantage point of what it means to have your money working harder for you. Let's look at an account that's going to be invested in stocks and say you get a 6 percent rate of return. When you take seventy-two and divide that by six, you get twelve. This means every twelve years your money will double. If you have a savings account that's getting 1 percent, seventy-two divided by one is seventy-two. So that means every seventy-two years, your money will double. Not good, right? A low-interest savings account has its place, and that place is an emergency fund or for your short-term goals. That is why it's so important to understand your time horizon and set clear goals when you invest.

Retirement Savings

Let's talk a little bit more about retirement savings. Everyone has a different definition for retirement. I've heard some people say they would like to retire "like yesterday," while some say, "I will never retire." How you view retirement is personal, but I do believe in making sure you have something to show for your future self no matter where you stand. You never know what will happen in the future, and giving yourself options is key to financial freedom.

Retirement savings are the part of financial wellness pertaining to your future. First, it's important to understand how much is enough for you. I believe this is a question you must ask throughout your financial wellness journey. I have a simple rule of thumb, called the Rule of 40, to provide you a high-level view of your retirement savings needs (It doesn't include inflation, precisely).

Ask yourself, what do I need to spend in today's dollars to live the lifestyle that I want to live when I retire? Multiply that annual amount by forty. For example, you may want $70,000 per year to live a good life. Of course, this number is after the house and debts are paid off. Multiply $70,000 times forty. The result is $2,800,000. On the other hand, you may say that you can live off $40,000 per year and be perfectly fine. Then, using the Rule of 40, you can say that you'll need to save close to $1,600,000.

Again, the number is unique to you and it's just a rule of thumb that doesn't include taxes or inflation. How does your present retirement savings compare to the number you want to reach? This is where you'll be able to start to set some goals and put some money away now. At first this number can seem daunting, but with the proper strategies in place you can begin to save little by little and watch it grow over time. Remember: Rome wasn't built in a day, and your retirement savings won't be either.

You need to utilize your work retirement plans such as your 401(k), which allow you to put away a certain amount every year. As of 2021, you may contribute $19,500 per year to your 401(k). If you are over fifty years old, you may contribute an additional $6,500 for what is known as a "catch up contribution." You get to automate those contributions, so they go into your retirement account every paycheck. I recommend that you increase your savings rate every year so you are saving as much as possible. In addition, as you get raises, increase your savings rate. In the book *Nudge*, Richard Thaler and Cass Sunstein discuss a program idea called the Save More Tomorrow program. In this program, it shows that employees who agree to increase their retirement plan contribution by 3 percent with each raise were able to quadruple their savings rate to 13.6 percent over the course of three and a half years and four pay raises.

Social Security

Another aspect of your retirement savings is social security. Visit ssa.gov to pull your social security statement. Now, some people don't believe they're ever going to get social security, but we don't know for sure. Therefore, it's good to be aware of what is available. Social security income is not designed to be retirement, but it can offset any income you may need for retirement to keep the lifestyle you desire.

Action Provoking Exercise

- Do you have an emergency fund?
- How would life be better for you if you had your emergency fund?
- What value most closely aligns with having an emergency fund?
- What is a comfortable retirement for you?
- Take a moment to pull your social security statement on ssa.gov. What did you observe?
- Do the goals that you have align with your investment vehicles?
- What changes need to be made?
- What money bucket do you feel needs the most attention from you?
- How can you make your three money buckets harmonize with each other?

CHAPTER 7

OWE NO MAN: FROM DEBT MANAGEMENT TO DEBT ELIMINATION

"Owe nothing to anyone—except for your obligation to love one another."

—ROMANS 13:8 NLT

From my earliest memories, I was uncomfortable owing money to anyone. As a first-year college student, I recall walking through the Oval, which is a beautiful green space with paths, trees, and grass, at my alma mater, The Ohio State University, and being enticed to get a free water bottle or dry erase board in exchange for a credit card application. Depending on what I wanted that day, I could be persuaded to apply by these cheap gimmicky temptations. I never planned to use the credit card because I was afraid of debt. However, it always baffled me that credit card companies would lure college students into debt when the majority of students didn't have a steady income. "A 2019 Sallie Mae survey found that approximately 30 percent of college students with more than $1,000 in credit card debt owed more than they did the previous month" (Irby 2019). For those who have become debt-ridden, this chapter will help you create a strategy to go from debt management to debt elimination. As the quote by Nathan Morris alludes to, the quicker you are out of debt, the sooner you can start saving money for yourself.

If you have debt, I want you to ask yourself: What would life be like if I had no debt? How does debt affect my daily life decisions?

Antoinette Munroe

Antoinette Munroe is a great example of staying focused on becoming debt-free. I mentioned her in the chapter on net worth as well. Even though she received some scholarships for attending Florida A & M University, she still had some student loan debt for completing her fifth and final year of college. She graduated with a bachelor's and a master's degree on December 28, 2008. Right after graduation, she got a corporate job with Pepsi. Pepsi gave her the highest job offer, so that was the main catalyst for her decision.

Pepsi opened a whole new world for her. She went from having taken maximum three vacations all her life to traveling the world with her new corporate job. She had an expense account, which allowed her to try new foods and experience a completely different life than the one she grew up in. She recalls that the fast food two-dollar menu was her food staple as a high schooler. With limited funds as a teenager, she didn't venture outside of the food she was used to because she knew that if she didn't like it, she wouldn't be able to buy anything else. Now that she had a corporate job, she was able to test out new foods on the company's dime.

Soon after starting her job, she started studying financial gurus like Clark Howard, Dave Ramsey, and Suze Orman to develop a budgeting system and debt elimination strategy that worked for her. She never really wanted to work for anyone, but she had incurred $32,000 in debt. She determined that she needed to pay off her debt in two years and then build up $50,000 in savings to live her dream.

She was very diligent about understanding what her expenses were per week and changing her billing dates so that it worked better with her lifestyle. This focus didn't come without great sacrifice—everyone around her was taking cruises and trips. She quickly learned that they were taking these vacations while having student loan debt. Their focus was not like hers. Debt elimination wasn't a priority for them. She didn't go out to eat a lot because it wasn't in her budget. She was willing to make the sacrifice to her social life to achieve her goals.

After paying off student loan debt in two years, she was ready to move closer to home and start to build her $50,000 savings goal. She received a promotion from her employer and moved home to Miami. She negotiated with her parents to move back home and not pay rent in the first year to minimize her expense obligations. During that entire year of living rent free, she gave herself $400 per month for her living expenses like gas and food. Every other dollar from her salary went toward her savings goal. After that year was up, she negotiated to start paying $400 in rent per month so that she could work toward meeting her goals.

She was very disciplined in her approach to achieving her goals. In addition to the "therapy" she practiced in the net worth chapter, she also had a rule that if she bought something and didn't wear it in thirty days, she had to return it. What realistic rules can you give yourself to ensure you are meeting your goals? (i.e., return items if not worn in thirty days, sleep on any financial decisions over $75, call an accountability buddy if you want to spend over $150, etc.). By the time she received her Miami promotion, she says her salary was at least $60,000. She was diligent about keeping her expenses low and not using her salary increases to spend more. Instead, she used her salary increases to save more. She ended up reaching her goal of saving $50,000 in one year.

When I think of Antoinette's success, the first thing that comes to mind is sacrifice. She was able to eliminate debt and save due to sacrifice. Of course, not everyone has the opportunity to move back home, which was such a blessing in accelerating her savings plan, but we all can take a deeper look at our spending to see where we can sacrifice to reach our financial goal of debt freedom. She also used the promotion and the increase in income to keep herself on track toward her goals.

The term "lifestyle creep" refers to how, as we increase our income, our expenses increase. How is it that we were able to survive on the lower salary but as our income increases, we wonder, where did the money go? That's lifestyle creep.

Many times, we believe we "deserve it." We believe that we've worked hard, so why not treat ourselves. I believe that it's important to celebrate your milestones and wins. It doesn't mean that you have to "celebrate" in perpetuity. Reward yourself and go back to the plan.

A way to avoid lifestyle creep is to understand your cash flow management. Refer to more about cash flow management in the chapter entitled "The Better Rainy Days…" "Easily accessible credit and the use of credit cards, which enable bigger purchases, may contribute to lifestyle creep," according to an Investopedia article entitled "Lifestyle Creep."

Some other examples as pointed out in the article include:

- Spending several dollars per day on coffee
- Flying premium economy rather than coach
- Eating out frequently and more expensively
- Expensive clothing (and more of it when less expensive clothing will suffice)
- Buying or renting more house than you need (or a second home)
- A third car, a boat, or replacing a car sooner than you need to

As we consider financial wellness and its benefits, I would like you to become familiar with debt management (Spoiler alert: as much as it is in your control, stop using your credit cards!). I believe in overall financial wellness, which means, to me, having a healthy, stress-free, anxiety-free relationship with money.

Part of financial wellness is understanding your debt. I believe debt causes you to experience stress. Become financially well by taking care of your mountain of debt. Since interest rates are at an all-time low at the time of writing this book, proactively call your credit card companies to see if you can lower the interest rate on your credit card. Take the time to ask questions about all the offers they have and compare that to what works for your budget.

You may even consider a balance transfer. A balance transfer is when you transfer the credit card balance from one credit card company to another to get a lower interest rate or even a 0 percent interest rate in the hopes of paying off your debt sooner and, hopefully, saving money. The balance transfer is not free. Many credit card companies will charge a percentage of your balance so that you can get the lower interest rate. The percentage they charge can be as low as 3 percent and as high as 5 percent. According to the Investopedia article "How Credit Card Balance Transfers Work," you may even be able to negotiate this transfer fee to make the transfer more economical.

Another aspect of the balance transfer is that there is usually a lower interest rate on the funds that you transfer from the other credit card company. For instance, the new credit card company may offer you the opportunity to transfer the balance at a 0 percent interest for eighteen months and after the promotional period is over your interest rate will go up. You need to calculate the cost of the transfer and your ability to pay the money back during the lower rate period. Also, find out what the rate is when your promotion period ends because any balance you have left over after your promotion period ends can potentially set you back if it's too high. This option could be very detrimental to your overall debt elimination plan if you don't count the costs.

Next, putting together a strategy is important to achieving debt freedom. There are two techniques that I like to share. One is called the debt snowball and the other is the debt avalanche.

Here's how the debt snowball works:

1. Gather all your credit card statements.
2. List all your debts from the lowest balance to the highest balance on paper or in a spreadsheet.

3. Determine what the minimum payment is on each credit card.
4. Determine how much you are paying over the minimum payment on each card. If you are only paying the minimum payment, then decide how much you can add to the minimum payment.
5. Begin to apply the minimum payment plus your extra funds to the credit card with the lowest balance. You will continue to pay the minimum payment on all the other credit cards.
6. After you completely pay off the lowest balance, then apply the full payment you made to your first credit card to the next lowest balance.
7. You will continue until you pay all your credit cards off.

I enjoy this technique because it is organized, and you can see the progress that you're making. When you make progress, you celebrate your wins. With any financial goal you create, you should celebrate your win. By no means do I mean celebrate your win by doing more frivolous spending that may have gotten you into debt in the first place but take the time to reflect on this big win. Some ideas on how to celebrate your win without going back into debt would be to give yourself one latte that you gave up to reach this goal, take yourself out to dinner, make yourself your favorite dessert, use a percentage of your overall debt payoff balance to treat yourself to something nice (for example, if your debt balance was $10,000, you resolve that you'll give yourself one percent of the paid off balance to treat yourself to something nice. In this case, that would be $100 and only $100, nothing else), tell a friend, etc.

The point here is not to do something so extravagant that you go back into debt but to celebrate this milestone and create an action plan for achieving your next financial goal. Fortunately, whatever payments you were making toward your debt elimination plan can now be directed toward saving, investing, or other financial goals that you desire. With the debt snowball technique, you will see constant progress. It may take longer to complete but knowing that you're making progress will keep you encouraged along the way.

The other technique to consider is the debt avalanche technique. It's a similar concept to the debt snowball method. Instead of categorizing everything by the lowest balance, you are categorizing all your credit cards by the highest interest rate. Initially, you're going to pay as much as you can toward the credit card with the highest interest rate. You can use various tools like one offered by NerdWallet to complete the debt avalanche (O'Shea and Pyles 2021). You may also use NerdWallet to find out whether the debt snowball or debt avalanche is best for you. One of the things you'll find is that the debt avalanche can potentially be a less expensive way for you to pay off your debts. However, your milestones toward paying off your debts and your celebration opportunities are less frequent than the debt snowball. The best part about choosing either technique is that you can't lose—either way, you are tackling the mountain of debt.

Now is a good time to pull your credit report. That's another aspect that you want to focus on. Every year we are offered a free credit report, and there are a lot of sites out there that will offer the credit report, however I only recommend the one by the Federal Trade Commission on a page by the name of "Get My Free Credit Report." This way you can ensure that you are receiving your free credit report from a reputable site. You should not pay for your credit report, either.

I recommend you pull your credit report throughout the year. There are three credit reporting agencies: Experian, Equifax, and TransUnion. Starting today, pull your Experian credit report. Four months from today, pull Equifax, and then four months from that point pull TransUnion. You may pull them in any order. This way you are monitoring your credit throughout the year. This is a great strategy for you to be able to get out of debt and gain peace of mind.

Becoming debt-free takes discipline, consistency, and motivation. Without discipline, you will find yourself in a vicious cycle of debt.

In this chapter, I mostly talked about consumer debt, however, one can get into debt due to unforeseen medical circumstances. "According to a 2016 Kaiser Family and *New York Times* study, 1 in 4 Americans has trouble paying a recent medical bill" (*Single Care (Blog)* 2021). "The *American Journal of Medicine* reports that nearly half of people who experience medical bankrupcy named hospital bills as their biggest expense" (*Single Care (Blog)* 2021). In Chapter 5, I discussed risk management and why it's important to create a plan for unforeseen circumstances such as medical issues.

Action Provoking Exercise

- What pressures do you feel keep you from becoming debt-free? (i.e., peer pressure, bills, income deficit, etc.)
- What strategy will you employ to become debt-free: debt avalanche or the debt snowball?
- If you have debt, I want you to ask yourself: what would life be like if I had no debt?
- How does debt affect my daily life decisions?

CHAPTER 8

START WITH WHAT YOU HAVE

"How many millionaires do you know who have become wealthy by investing in savings accounts? I rest my case."

—ROBERT G. ALLEN

My name is Sena. But they are calling me "wench" as I stand here in humiliation being put on display for these evil men to bid on me and purchase me. How humiliating! How did I get here? How does one human purchase another? This has to be a nightmare that I will soon awaken from. The monster who is about to purchase me can't be human. I can't be bought. He may purchase my body but not my spirit or soul. This is the inner conversation I imagine a recently enslaved African woman using as they stand before enslavers in 1711 on the corner of Pearl and Wall Streets. This location in Manhattan is near where Wall Street is located today (Boyd 2016).

Before we get into investing strategies, it's important to note the history of the stock market. It wasn't until I was much older that I began to make the connection between the stock market and enslavement. Since enslaved Africans were not considered humans, it's no mistake that humans were being bought and sold just like shares of company stock were being sold not too far from the New York Stock Exchange. It's mind-boggling to me to understand that my ancestors were treated as property and sold. I still can't quite comprehend it, but it's real and it happened. "Slavery was officially abolished in the US in 1865, but historians say the legacy of slavery cannot be untangled from its economic impact," says Zoe Thomas (Thomas 2019). We cannot separate the two. In New York's Financial District you can find the site of one of the United States' largest slave markets. It is located just two streets away from the current site of the New York Stock Exchange. If one were to look at anything historical in this country, they'd soon realize that it was built from back-breaking cruel labor for free! The tie between American economic history and enslavement history is astounding. "Enslaved people were brought to work on the cotton, sugar, and tobacco plantations. The crops they grew were sent to Europe or to the northern colonies, to be turned into finished products. Those finished goods were used to fund trips to Africa to obtain more slaves who were then trafficked back to America. This triangular trading route was profitable for investors," says Zoe Thomas (Thomas 2019). Once we realize the connection of slavery to investing, then we can see why many Black Americans have not invested or may have a fear of investing. "Among middle-aged families—who have the highest rates of account ownership—Sixty-five percent of White families have at least one retirement account, compared to forty-four percent of Black families," the Fed said (Bhutta et al. 2020).

While living in Phoenix, I attended a get-together at a friend's home. Many of my friends and acquaintances knew that I worked in the financial services industry. At this time, I was working for a big financial services company and had not started working with individual investors. However, since I was in the industry, people asked me questions about investing or the market. At this get-together, I distinctly remember someone saying to me that investing in the stock market might as well be like gambling. Again, I wasn't providing investment advice to individuals at this time, but I wanted her to know that it was different from gambling. However, it was hard to convince someone who believed this way, so I never tried to argue. Although investing is risky, it is a strategy for building wealth. I do believe that many people, especially Black Americans, shy away from it. I want to share some strategies for investing and these principles are foundational when it comes to taking the time to invest.

Mellody Hobson's Story

Mellody Hobson is the president and co-CEO of Ariel Investments. Ariel Investments, founded by John W. Rogers, Jr., in 1983, is a Black-owned investment company located in Chicago. Mellody is the youngest of her family of six children. The difference in age between her oldest sister and Mellody is twenty-five years. She grew up with a single mom who was struggling. She said it was difficult. She remembers her mom going to a gas station to ask the gas attendant if they could borrow $5 worth of gas in order to get her to school.

She also remembers her mom making bad financial decisions, such as buying her kids Easter dresses and clothes instead of paying the phone bill. However, she knew that at the end of the day her mother would do anything for her. She never had that concern.

Considering her experiences, Mellody doesn't think it's an accident that she works in the financial industry "because as a child she was desperate to understand money" ("Financial Literacy: Mellody Hobson at TEDxMidwest" 2014). She attended great schools and she got an internship at Ariel Investments while attending Princeton University. When she started there, she didn't know anything about investing. To this day, she is baffled, as too am I, that the majority of US schools will teach "about wood shop or auto and no class on investing." It's mind-boggling since everyone will have to manage money at some point in their lives. It's a given.

Mellody's first job after graduation was at Ariel Investments. She started at the bottom of the corporate ladder at Ariel, and her starting salary was $35,000. She was so excited to create financial stability for herself. With this new job, she could pay her rent and her phone bills. Even though she knew her salary wasn't a lot, she says, "It was enough." She decided that she was going to live her life very differently from how she grew up and that she "would take responsibility for herself financially so that she would never experience that level of insecurity."

Mellody immersed herself in books and magazines to get inspired. She remembers reading a quote from *Cosmopolitan* magazine by Judy Collins, a folk singer from the 1960s, which read, "As women we are raised to have rescue fantasies, and I'm here to tell you that no one is coming." What a saying. I think it makes us think about what we can do to change our narrative even when we think about the wrongs that need to be corrected for Black Americans who are descendants of enslaved people in the US. What if things continue as they are, and the debt America owes never gets paid?

Well, in the meantime, we will overcome as we always have, and we will build generational wealth legacies.

Mellody took that quote and resolved in her mind that she would save, invest, and work to create the life she dreamed for herself. She was able to draw from her mother's independent spirit. Her mom, being a single mother, worked very hard and was a believer that anything is possible.

Along with living a life of independence and taking control of her life, Mellody was impacted by a saying by Neil Simon: "If no one ever took any risks, Michelangelo would have painted the Sistine floor." As we know, he painted a beautiful fresco on the ceiling of the Sistine Chapel, which you can still visit today. What a feat. Mellody labels Michelangelo's painting the Sistine Chapel as taking a risk. Taking risk is difficult but so is not taking a risk. She explains that when it comes to investing, the "stock market has outperformed all other investments over the long term." I always tell people that the stock market can do three things: it can go up, it can go down, or it can remain flat. The problem is that I don't know when that will happen. That's what concerns people about investing, but there are strategies. They don't guarantee results but can help you make educated decisions about how to invest your money.

Another quote that Mellody references is a Winston Churchill quote: "If you are going through hell, keep going." Mellody remembers she and her family being kicked out of their home as child and thinking to herself that she can't wait until she gets big so that she could make sure this situation doesn't happen to her. I like the Churchill statement, too, because it reminds me that we just need to press through our challenges. In the words of a song that my church choir would sing on Sunday mornings, "Trouble don't last always." It's true. Just keep pushing forward. We all have to start somewhere when it comes to investing and in life. I'm reminded by the saying, "Despise not, small beginnings," which is found in Zechariah 4:10. It's okay to start small—we all must start somewhere and build from there.

"Do what you can, with what you've got, where you are," President Theodore Roosevelt said. And for Mellody, that meant to give. She believes giving is just as important as making money. She loves to help people make money so that they can give it away. I agree that giving is also a way to invest, and I have a whole chapter dedicated to giving in this book. Mellody and John Rogers have a school called Ariel Community Academy where they give first grade classes on the south side of Chicago $20,000 to invest. They have a giving, saving, and investing component to the funds, and each student learns principles about money in conjunction with giving to the next class of students behind them and receiving some of the funds for their education. It sounds like a phenomenal program that gives real world financial literacy lessons (Koval 2019).

Mellody decided to live her life as if no one were coming to save her, and now she is the executive at a major corporation. In December 2020, she was named the chairwoman of Starbucks corporation, "making her one of the highest-profile Black directors in corporate America" (Ludlow 2020).

Save Consistently

Mellody Hobson is a brilliant example of why we must start with what we have. There's no get-rich-quick formula; however, it's important to implement strategies. One such strategy is to save consistently. Whether you are saving or investing, it's a great idea to automate your savings. I have a few subscription services, and what I like is that I know that I will have items come to me on a consistent basis. For instance, for household staples like laundry detergent, I have a subscription. Every three to four months, I get a new box of detergent pods. I am assured that I won't run out and I don't have to be concerned about making a trip to the store to get it. I am not a fan of shopping, so this service works well for me. I also have a cell phone and it's on a subscription. Every month the bill is paid automatically. The cell phone company is happy because they are assured to receive the payment, and I am happy because I don't have to remember to pay another bill. Just like anything it is important to check periodically to make sure you are not incurring charges that shouldn't be there.

This same process and philosophy can very easily be completed with your own finances. There's a saying that states, "Pay yourself first." I am a big proponent of that. Why not create a subscription account for yourself, which would be a savings account. You will be paying yourself and prioritizing your goals. You should also do this for your investing as well.

In investing, this is called systematic investing. You can determine a dollar amount that you want to save every month and the funds that you put into the account—whether it is a taxable brokerage account or a retirement account—will be invested in the vehicle of your choice. I like the systematic investing or dollar-cost averaging strategy because you can take the emotion out of investing by making purchases at various prices throughout the year but using the same dollar amount on the same day of the month to make the investment. It's automated so it's not set it and forget it, but it is set it and monitor it. You'll want to keep an eye throughout the year on your accounts so you know what is happening. It's really important to prioritize ourselves when it comes to money, and it is okay to pay yourself just like you pay your bills. Again, you have to start somewhere. The younger you start the better it'll be; however, you can start at whatever age you are.

If you have fluctuating income, you can still do systematic investing, but you will have to be more manual in your method. Doing it manually will take more oversight and discipline but always go back to your values and your why, and it'll keep you motivated. Set an appointment with yourself every month or whenever you pay your bills to assess if you are able to save that month and how much you are able to save. If you save fifty dollars a month for twenty years at a 6 percent rate of return, you will have $23,102.87. Imagine if you saved $500 a month for twenty years at a 6 percent rate of return—you would have $231,028.68.

If you are saving for retirement you can save in a few vehicles. A Roth IRA or a traditional IRA in 2021 allow you to save a max of $6,000 per year and, if you are over fifty years old, you can save an additional $1,000, which is called the "catch-up." The Roth IRA requires salary eligibility and it's best to refer to irs.gov to understand the limitations and eligibility for your situation. If you work for an employer that offers a retirement plan like the 401(k) you may even contribute $19,500 annually and you can add a "catch up" contribution over fifty years old of $6,500 in 2021. If you are eligible to save in a Roth IRA, then this is the type of vehicle that you can save $500 per month into.

The other benefit of doing systematic investing is to help alleviate emotional investing.

Emotional investing causes you to get in and out of the market at the wrong times and thus do market timing. If you pick a date every month and a dollar amount to invest, you have a higher chance of staying invested, and you'll also avoid market timing.

As you start with what you have, you can steadily increase your savings so that you can reach your goals. I recommend taking advantage of your company retirement plan to increase your savings percentage by 1 percent every year at a minimum. That way if you are getting raises on an annual basis, you will automatically prioritize your savings goals. If the company doesn't offer an automatic savings increase, then you have to be vigilant about doing it yourself—but, again, this is the opportunity to save more for your future self.

Recently, I have recognized this trend that instead of celebrating a birthday for one day, many are taking the whole month to celebrate. It's a great way to commemorate living one more year on this Earth. If you are one to celebrate your birthday for a month, add increasing your savings as an activity, especially if you don't have it automated. Every year you will set an appointment with your financial advisor or yourself or someone in your circle of trusted friends and make sure that you increase your savings by a percentage or a dollar amount. Remember you are paying yourself so it's a win-win.

Many people ask what they should have saved for retirement by a certain age, and it's a really hard question because everyone's retirement lifestyle is different, and everyone's life expectancy is different too. I highly recommend having this conversation with a financial planner for a more tailored plan. However, for those who want to know if you're saving enough, I read an article on Fidelity's website that provides some helpful milestones. "Fidelity's rule of thumb: Aim to save at least 1x your salary by 30, 3x by 40, 6x by 50, 8x by 60, and 10x by 67" ("How Much do I Need to Retire?" 2020).

Julia Collins: Finding the Joy in Your Money

Meet Julia Collins, who was born and raised in San Francisco, California. Julia has a strong connection to family. In fact, her grandfather moved to San Francisco during the Great Migration. The Great Migration was a time during which Black Americans left the oppression of the Jim Crow South to seek a better life for their families between 1917 and 1970 ("The Great Migration" 2021).

Growing up, I knew that my family's roots were in Alabama and North Carolina and didn't fully grasp that they moved to the North (mainly Ohio) due to the Great Migration, fleeing the Jim Crow terrorism of the South in hope for better opportunities. Julia's grandfather was a dentist in San Francisco, and he helped everyone regardless of their skin complexion. Because of that, her family became a center of the community. Whenever her family and friends would gather, they would do so around delicious food. Food was a love language to welcome people, be hospitable, and show love.

She had her son at thirty-nine years old, and during that time of postpartum, she experienced a time to "reframe and rethink… see things with fresh eyes." As she started to raise her son, she became "deeply concerned about the condition of people living on the planet." She was aware of the relationship between food and climate change, but when she learned that "25 percent of all global greenhouse gas emissions was coming from land use and food systems," she became incredibly angry. She realized that when African and Native Americans were in charge of the land, this was not an issue.

The method of farming that started in the US since the 1940s is taking a heavy toll on our land and climate. Armed with this information, Julia became extremely angry. Then she started to look in her own home and "began to imagine what it would look like if every product in her household was climate friendly." So it's no surprise that Julia is the owner of a company called Planet Forward, which has a "mission to combat climate change by reducing greenhouse emissions through regenerative agriculture."

Under Planet Forward, she has created her first food company to combat climate change called Moonshot. Moonshot creates healthy snacks while keeping in mind who and where the ingredients are coming from. Moonshot was created to build a "climate friendly brand [so that] she could raise her son on a healthy planet." Through her business and awareness about how food affects our climate, she has embarked on a journey to make changes in her household steps at a time. She noted that she is not perfect and is still in the process of even making changes around her home as it's part of the journey.

Julia was quick to connect this journey and process to our money mindset and finding the joy in developing a healthy relationship with money. She pointed out that we must let go of this need to feel perfect. Julia describes herself as someone who is now "in touch with money. Meaning that I'm in conversation with money and in contract with money and in relationship to money." She said this wasn't always the case in her twenties and thirties. She was detached and out of relationship with it. She just didn't want to embody the responsibility that comes with wealth generation. She was in this "insidious cycle of work and spend." She noted that the "work and spend" term came from Thorstein Veblen, author of *The Theory of the Leisure Class*, a book written in 1899 focusing on human institutions, both social and economic, "that shape society, such as how the citizens earn their livelihoods, wherein technology and the industrial arts are the creative forces of economic production." From the "work and spend" mentality, she realized she has a lot of avoidance where she didn't want to check balances on her accounts or create a budget. So with that, she created this rollercoaster of not spending anything and then going through periods of spending.

Julia wasn't in balance, and she is someone who finds her "joy in a balanced state." Therefore, she was never in a "place of joy" because she was not balanced. She was on this rollercoaster of a ride with money. On the other hand, she understood that she has a healthy relationship with her body. For example, she is aware of her exercise routine, and she is aware of how she eats. She is aware of her capacity for joy and pleasure in her body, which means she is in harmony with her body most of the time.

As she began to generate more wealth through her work and she started to get more inflow, it triggered opportunity for her. Therefore, she had a "greater capacity for wealth generation." She had an "aha moment" where she decided that she should develop a relationship with money in a similar way to her relationship with her body and her physical well-being. She decided to do a financial assessment like how she assessed her health. She began to ask the questions, "Where am I with my financial health?" and "Where am I with my credit?" After working with a financial advisor, she dispelled the myth in her mind that she had to have $10 million of liquid income before she could work with an advisor.

At this point, with the help of her financial advisor, who became a trusted friend, she began to make a plan to get out of the "insidious cycle of work and spend" and she began to assume that she would continue to generate wealth, thus moving out of a restriction mindset to an abundance mindset. She decided to have a healthy relationship with money once she realized how being a good steward over her finances would lead to more blessings.

Julia shared that she is not perfect and, just like you, can fall off track with exercising and then get back on track. She has had to do the same with money. For example, when the news is headlining scary stories about the stock market, she can get into the scarcity mindset, but it's brief and she gets back on track. She attributes that to her "personal power recipe," which is "staying in her joy" where she is creative and doing what she needs to do to be a good leader and resilient.

Julia loves to take inventory and, from time to time, she'll take an inventory of where "joy shows up in [her] life." Being in a scarcity mindset, fear, and shame are all things that rob her of her joy, power, and effectiveness. From this exercise, she has determined that an abundance mindset is a strategic business imperative because that is where she can stay in her joy.

Action Provoking Exercise

- Our mindsets are so key in reaching a place of satisfaction in our relationship with money.
    - How is your relationship with money? Excellent, Good, Needs Improvement, Bad
    - How can you release perfectionism and be in a state of joy?
    - What problem were you put on Earth to solve?

SECTION 4

GIVE

"Alone we can do so little; together, we can do so much."
—HELEN KELLER

As I mentioned in the introduction, I want to dispel the myth that one must pull themselves up by their own bootstraps in order to create and generate wealth. I have found that whenever I set out to accomplish something, I am most successful when I have a community. Community doesn't have to be a particular number of people. Even one additional person can help you reach your goal or goals.

When I attended The Ohio State University, one of my roommates and I decided to work on our health goals. She solicited the help of a friend who was great at lifting weights. He took the time to share with us the importance of good form when lifting, how many reps to do, and which exercises we should do. Basically, he gave us a workout. My roommate and I made sure that we incorporated our workouts into our weekly schedule while both of us juggled the rigor of the engineering coursework. We were extremely devoted, and we started to see results. If it wasn't for the fact that we were supporting each other and holding each other accountable, we would not have achieved the success we were seeking in our fitness goals.

I always hear people say that growing up, their parents didn't talk about finances. Many adults I have spoken to over the years say that they don't talk about it among themselves either. Of course, we constantly hear that it is not taught in schools. Having a safe community with which to talk about finances can help us all move forward faster in the quest of our financial goals.

You have a 65 percent chance of completing a goal if you commit to someone that you will do it. It's also encouraging to note that if you have a specific accountability appointment with someone you've committed to, you will increase your chance of success by up to 95 percent (Newland 2018). Accountability requires us to involve our community so that we can achieve the goals and success that we seek.

In this section, we'll discuss goals, the importance of accountability and why you should tell people you trust about your goal. My hope is that the activities and exercises will help you achieve real results.

CHAPTER 9

YOUR FINANCIAL SUCCESS STORY

Write Your Financial Success Story

What if we got a video every year of all the activities and accomplishments of our lives? At the end of every year, Facebook gives me a summary of everything that I posted throughout the year. It's the "highlight reel" of my life. If you're on Facebook, you may have received this as well. Have you ever thought about what you'd change or add to it to make it come out just as you'd like?

I believe that everyone has a financial success story that they would like to create. Perhaps, you've already crafted your story. I like to look at our financial lives as a book. Each stage of our financial story consists of chapters. With any book, you should have a beginning, a middle and an end. Every book has a first chapter and a last chapter. The first chapter of your financial life has been written, but the last has not. There's power in your last chapter because you can now control the narrative.

In 2004, I took the Dale Carnegie Leadership course. We learned to be courageous by sharing our goals with the entire class. The power was in sharing them out loud in front of a group of people. We had to give a lot of thought to what goal we were going to share. Not only did the group hear us share it, but we heard ourselves share it. We believed our goal. When you share your goals in front of a group you make an extra effort to accomplish the goal because you want to be a man or woman of your word. It's called accountability. If you're like me, you won't share such an important goal unless you plan to do it.

Another powerful aspect of this exercise is that we had to take the time to visualize the day we accomplished the goal. We had to share where we were. If it was six months from today, we took the time to look at the day of the week this goal was accomplished. We imagined where we were when we accomplished the goal. We spoke in the present. Someone might say, "Today is July 1, 2023. It's a Monday and it's very sunny and I'm sitting on my patio reflecting on how great God is as I have accomplished my goal of starting my new Etsy business selling handcrafted bridal gown dresses. I'm extremely excited because I am processing ten orders, which is double what I anticipated at this time."

In the year I took this class, I shared something like this: "It's Monday, October 4, 2004, and I'm so excited because I have changed careers from engineering sales to financial services. I'm loving this new role because it is in line with my passion to help others achieve financial literacy. In addition, I purchased my first duplex where I live in one unit and rent out the other unit." Sharing this goal with the audience, I felt they were rooting for me, and I also felt the power of saying it out loud to them. I didn't have a personal relationship with anyone in my class, but I made sure whatever I decided to say was backed up by conviction and a keen sense that I truly wanted to accomplish these goals that I set. By sharing and visualizing where I was and the day of the week with the date that I accomplished the goal, it felt more real. I actually believed it could come to pass.

Wouldn't you know that within six to eight months, all the things that I shared happened. They didn't happen on the exact day that I predicted, but my career change occurred a few months before the date. I changed careers and started my new job in financial services on September 7, 2004. I couldn't even sleep that whole Labor Day weekend because I was so excited about starting my new career. My duplex was under contract in December 2004 and closed in January 2005. It was a phenomenal exercise.

My first "money memory" goes back to when I was a little girl. I believe I was eight years old. I was so excited because my father gave my sisters and me twenty dollars each so that we could buy Christmas Gifts. It really seemed like a lot of money to me at the time. I had two sisters and my mom and dad to purchase Christmas gifts for. I'm the oldest, and my sisters were six and two years old at that time. I distinctly recall doing all my Christmas shopping at Woolworth. Being that I was just learning math, I knew that I had five dollars for each family member. I remember purchasing powder for my mother. It was in either a clear blue or pink container with a cushiony applicator. I don't remember what I purchased for everyone else, but I was very proud of the fact that I purchased a gift for everyone with money to spare. I was so happy, in fact, that I came home to tell my dad that I was able to buy all my Christmas gifts with the money he gave me and had some savings left over. He encouraged me and said, "That's great." That's my first money memory. From that point forward, I knew that saving money was a good thing.

Your first money memory is an important part of your backstory. We can use it to show how we were triumphant over challenges that came our way. We can use our backstory to propel us into our future. The backstory can be the source of our convictions as to why we're so passionate about our financial success story. Remember: you are the hero of your financial success story, and the backstory reveals what drives you to be victorious.

Now, I would like you to consider the last chapter of your financial success story. I know that it can seem a little morbid thinking of your last chapter, but one thing I can guarantee is that we will all have one. We just don't know when. So, if you were to take the time to write the last chapter of your financial success story, what would we read? Where are you? What are you doing? What did you accomplish? Who is with you? How old are you? What do you want to be remembered for? Where do you live? Where did you travel to? How many books did you read? Who did you help? How many businesses did or do you have? Did you buy the plane you always wanted? Did you take those piano lessons? Did you write your book or books? Did you get that degree? Did you start that charity or charities? Did you join that organization? Did you maintain that healthy lifestyle? Did you buy that vacation property that your family can use whenever they need it? Did you paint those portraits? Did you take that art class?

As you can see, the questions you can answer and write about in your last chapter are endless. I find that there's so much we want to do and accomplish, but day-to-day life can sidetrack us from staying focused on what we want our legacy to be. Some of the situations we find ourselves in today make it hard to even visualize accomplishing those dreams. But today, I want to help you remove those limitations.

First, I ask: What would you want to do if money was no object? How much is enough for you today? I believe everyone has their own definition of what that is or means to them. If there were no limits, how would you make sure your last chapter was written the way you want? Now I submit to you that you can believe. I submit that today is the day that you can insert a plot twist if the circumstances you find yourself in today don't line up with how you want your last chapter to read. You don't have to accept the narrative that has been written for your life thus far as what life will be like forever.

I am a believer in God and speaking out about what you want to see. I believe our words have power. We are bombarded with so many negative words every day. Since I am a believer in the Bible, I understand that we have to cast down imaginations and every high thing that exalts itself against the knowledge of God according to 2 Corinthians 10:5. In 2019, I was studying intensely for the Certified Financial Planner Exam. It was my hardest undertaking since my five years pursuing an electrical and computer engineering degree from The Ohio State University. It is a six-hour exam. I had to recall information from memory on any of the seven subjects including ethics, education planning and financial planning, estate planning, tax planning, investment planning, insurance planning, and retirement planning. The test had 170 questions and one to two case studies, and I had to recall the content and answer each question in a ninety-second window of time. It's quite intense and nerve-racking.

I share this to provide an example of the many times that I would hear these negative thoughts go through my head saying, "This is too hard." "What if you fail?" "Do they really want me to memorize this information?" "This information is out of touch with the real world." All these thoughts were set up to distract me from achieving my goal of passing the exam. The thoughts were trying to trap me into thinking that all of this wasn't necessary. However, I knew what I wanted and needed to accomplish, and I knew that I needed to cast down those thoughts and replace them with a positive, powerful thought that disputed and overthrew my doubts.

I started to speak the overruling confession or affirmation out loud during my practice and study time. This practice helped me to overcome the negative thoughts generated while I was taking the exam. During the exam, I found myself writing on my scratch paper something positive when I heard something negative. I don't remember exactly what I wrote but it was something like, "You can do all things through Christ who strengthens you" or "You are passing this exam." You can use a scripture, a positive saying, or quote that resonates with you and virtually annihilate and replace the thought that was counter to what you are setting out to accomplish.

Take the time to write out your personal financial success story. Start by writing what you want the ending to be. This is a great exercise for going beyond what you see for your life today—especially if what you see today is not what you want. You can create a plot twist that shows how the story changes because you overcame that challenge. I believe the process of writing your story, starting from the place that you aspire to be, can broaden your imagination. Give it a try. See where your imagination will take you.

Meet Jerome Revish

Jerome Revish is from my hometown, Columbus, Ohio. Since I grew up in Columbus, Ohio, I remember his father was a local news anchor. I can't forget that name since the memories of having a Black news anchor are so rare.

Jerome Revish is an executive at Cardinal Health. "Headquartered in Dublin, Ohio, Cardinal Health, Inc. (NYSE: CAH) is a distributor of pharmaceuticals, a global manufacturer and distributor of medical and laboratory products, and a provider of performance and data solutions for healthcare facilities" (Cardinal Health 2021). I want to highlight him as a corporate intrapreneur since most of my interviews and stories have been about entrepreneurs.

Again, community played a huge role in Jerome's life. One community that will probably have the most impact on our lives is our family. Jerome's first impression of a leader was his parents.

Growing up he saw his father work incredibly hard. He realized later in life that one of the lessons he learned from watching his father is "perseverance, that you aren't always going to be the first choice." He also realized that "faith plays an important part in how you view disappointment and success. Not getting too high in the highs and too low in the lows." His father would take him to business meetings, and that's where Jerome realized he wanted to be a leader and follow in his father's footsteps of becoming a servant leader.

Jerome also attributes his success to his immediate family, his wife and two daughters. Pre-COVID-19, he worked long late hours and would find himself on the road for most of the month. Both he and his wife are executives. Therefore, both he and his wife communicate constantly on their schedules to make sure they know who is going to be out of town and who is going to be in town. They work as a team and provide support and "build capacity for each other," says Jerome. His family has also been helpful in letting him know when they need him. For instance, when he's in a meeting, one of his daughters may call him while he is at work and respectfully ask, "Do you have five minutes?" He takes those subtle hints and clues to understand that it's time for him to spend more time with his daughters. His wife plays a pivotal role in communicating that as well to their children. Since the kids have gotten used to seeing their parents at home, he's very concerned that once things get back to normal "post-COVID," it might shake things up a bit.

Jerome's first memory about money was his first job at Kroger, one of the largest grocery stores in America. This job was the first time he earned money as opposed to receiving money. That first job taught him the joy of earning and the value of saving money. He also learned about how much money was taken out of his paycheck. To his amazement, he spent all this time working, but because of union dues, he felt like that first check was completely given away. He learned from that experience, "Everything you earn isn't yours." Because he started this job in high school, the lessons he learned inspired him to go to college so that he could develop a career, grow professionally, and make more money. He also learned that one job isn't going to be enough and started to do a side hustle. He said that very early on he started to develop small principles on saving. He opened a savings account. He recalls his mom taking him into the bank at five or six years old to open a savings account. He has passed this on to his daughters who are ten and twelve years old. Both have savings accounts and debit cards. They use the money from their accounts to make decisions on what they will buy and not buy. He's observed that one daughter is a big saver, and the other daughter is a big spender. These traits were displayed by them getting a small amount of money for themselves.

Given that both Jerome and his wife are executives with a finance background, they are blessed that money never became an argument for them because they were on the same page. He has a strong foundation of faith and spiritual habits with money. He looks at himself as a steward of the money. In consequence, he is mindful of why and where to spend. He's grown up in the church and has always been a consistent tither from when he started his first job. He has always tithed 10 percent of whatever he earned from the gross. From starting this habit at the age of fourteen, he said he's been "tremendously blessed."

Jerome doesn't want to be the only one doing well; therefore, he uses his money to give back to his church and his community, including family and friends. He said this is more common with Black executives because when Black people move up or make more money, they aren't just supporting themselves but supporting a niece, aunt, uncle, or parents. I actually call that the "Black tax." On the other hand, he says, "Our white counterparts oftentimes are having trusts set up for them or dad gives them this business," which is something we as Black Americans don't usually have. According to WeUnifyTech founder Thomas K. R. Stovall, "No one talks about the effect of what he calls the "reverse friends-and-family funnel" that some professionals of color struggle with, as mentioned in the article entitled "The hidden "black tax" that some professionals of color struggle with." In fact, "Black households annually earning between

$100,000 and $150,000 provided informal financial assistance in a given year at more than double the rate of their White peers" (Elliott, Kessel, Ndefo-Haven 2021).

Jerome is a Black executive whose official title is Senior Vice President at Cardinal Health, and unfortunately even today, being a Black executive at a corporation is rare. From the beginning of his career, he knew that he'd have to work twice as hard as others. Jerome experienced decent success early in his career. He said he was "Promoted pretty quickly and making what I thought was decent money." But as he moved up the ranks, he saw folks start to "lap him" and go faster than he did. He also noticed that he "didn't have a voice in the room because there weren't people that looked like me that thought like me that wanted to create opportunities for people like me." He also began to realize there were "People in the room who had biases both conscious and unconscious around Black leaders and Black men and being intimidated by a Black man. [They] had an expectation of, 'Can a Black man run this company, or can he run this department, or are these the functions that he should be in?'" Although Jerome has never experienced any overt racism, he says, "There are three Black men at his level or above and there is one Black woman at his level and three Black women VPs in his entire organization." Cardinal Health employs 48,000 employees, and the lack of Black executives is staggering.

After he shared the staggering statistics of the minuscule amount of Black leadership within his company, I had to ask him why he stays and doesn't pursue entrepreneurship. His answers were candid and honest. For one, he said, there's a comfort level in corporate America in that it "pays well." He also said there's a financial sacrifice and big leap with being an entrepreneur, especially when you have children. He knew that he'd have to have plenty of cash reserves so that he, his wife, and family didn't have to take a step back. He does understand that he still has some risk staying in corporate America because "someone else is his boss and they could impact him tomorrow." However, he's never been intrigued with running his own business. I love that perspective because entrepreneurship isn't for everyone and that's okay.

Jerome Revish is still making his impact by creating a strong financial legacy for his family and generations to come. He's placed himself in a position to define financial freedom for himself, which is "Not having to work, choosing to work. Being able to provide a legacy for the family. Being able to enjoy a comfortable lifestyle based on your personal desires. It doesn't necessarily mean you're out there as a billionaire on a private island. But whatever your personal lifestyle is… you can enjoy that. You don't work because you have to and you're able to provide that legacy. That's a good recipe for me of what financial freedom looks like."

Jerome and his wife are working to build financial freedom for their daughters not only by saving for college but also establishing what happens with their finances when they're gone. The other thing is assisting other family members, nephews, and nieces, for instance, and making sure they're setting them up well. He's a firm believer in giving his time and intellect by volunteering, giving advice, counsel, and support when necessary.

S.M.A.R.T.Y. Possibilities

Brainstorm All the Possibilities

In the 1980s and 1990s, an entire genre of book reading called "choose your own adventure" was popular. The genre was specifically targeted to boys and some girls ages seven to fourteen years old. In this genre, which was mainly written in second person, the main character, which was the reader, takes on the role of a doctor, spy, private investigator, or another type of protagonist. The format of the stories is such that the reader could choose from a number of scenarios that led to multiple endings depending on what was chosen. As a child, I don't remember reading such books, but they sound utterly engaging and entertaining for a reader.

We all know that how we come into the world is not our decision. For instance, we didn't choose our gender, ethnicity, culture, parents, country of citizenship, etc. So, if we were to look at our life as if it were a story, we didn't determine the beginning. However, I learned some lessons in life that led me to believe that we have a choice in our destination once we become an adult. When I was in my mid-twenties, I had a pastor who always said, "Life is choice-driven." This statement led me to believe that there's a good possibility we can determine the ending of our story.

I think that framing our financial story from this perspective can shed a lot of light on the narrative that we want to create. What if we could start at the end of our financial success story and then fill in the chapters in between to get as close as possible to creating the ending we want? I believe there are so many possibilities, and often we get caught up in the day-to-day, month-to-month, and year-to-year activities that we forget to take deliberate and initial actions toward all the possibilities that are available to us to make that phenomenal last chapter come true.

Create S.M.A.R.T.Y Possibilities (Goals)

Many professionals and students are familiar with the S.M.A.R.T goals acronym as an easy blueprint for creating solid goals for any area of our lives. Being a Financial Life-Planner Strategist myself, I have adopted the term "possibilities." I learned the importance of this term from a book written by Mitch Anthony and Paul Armson called *Life Centered Financial Planning: How to Deliver Value That Will Never Be Undervalued*. They challenge planners like me to swap out the term "goals" with the term "possibilities." I believe in order for us to live up to the beautiful last chapter of our winning financial success story, we must first think of all the possibilities ahead of us.

Therefore, I'm starting with the S.M.A.R.T.Y. possibilities. I recently added a "Y" to the S.M.A.R.T. Goals acronym, and I'll share more about that later in this section. Here's a reminder of what the acronym stands for:

S - Specific
M - Measurable
A - Attainable
R - Realistic
T - Timebound
Y - Why?

Since you've probably heard of this many times before, I'm going to point out a few aspects of this acronym so that you're able to look at it from a fresh perspective.

First, we'll review the various aspects of the acronym. The S stands for Specific. When we are creating our S.M.A.R.T.Y. possibilities, we need to start them by clearly identifying and defining them. Being precise in your goal setting possibilities will help you get closer to achieving them.

The "M" stands for measurable. A useful synonym is "numerable." Since we are referring to financial goals, the best way to make a S.M.A.R.T.Y. financial possibility measurable is to put numbers to it. We need to understand the dollars and cents that make this financial goal possible.

Next in this acronym is the A, which is Attainable. A synonym that stood out for me was the word Winnable. It's important to make sure your financial goals are Winnable and Attainable. You want to have something that encourages you to make progress even when roadblocks come your way. If the goal is winnable then you'll be motivated to get across the finish line. We have a high chance of having success and victory in that area when we look at all the attainable/winnable possibilities.

The next letter in the acronym is R, which stands for Realistic. According to the *Oxford Dictionary*, Realistic means having or showing a sensible and practical idea of what can be achieved or expected. It's important to make sure your goal is Realistic. I believe this goes hand in hand with Attainable. Having a realistic goal allows you to believe in your ability to accomplish that goal.

Now let's move on to the next letter in the acronym, the T, which stands for Time-bound.

Whenever you start a race, you're aware that there is a finish line. The time-bound portion of this acronym is that you will actually put a date to when you want to accomplish the goals you have set. Having a set date gives you a deadline and creates a sense of urgency to accomplish your goals. I enjoy the quote by Milton Erickson: "A goal without a date is just a dream."

Now the reason my acronym is slightly different from what you've seen before is because I added a Y. The Y actually stands for Why. The "Why" is going to be the reason for reaching your possibilities. It's going to be your motivation for achieving your goal. When you dig deep into your Why, nothing will stop you from achieving the possibilities you've set forth. It may not happen exactly in the time frame you determine or precisely the way you want, but that Why is going to be the driving force behind achieving what you've set out to do.

Of course, in addition to making winnable goals, it's also important to make sure they are worth winning.

Create progress points for evaluating your goals. If it's a five-year goal, monitor it every quarter. If it's a three-month goal check it every week. Then after you perform your periodic check-ups, remember to celebrate your wins.

Celebrating your accomplishments is so important to your overall financial success. You know how disciplined you were while you were pursuing your goals. You remember the sacrifice you made and the things you gave up to reach your possibilities. You need to acknowledge that and celebrate. I highly recommend deciding how you want to celebrate your achievements when you create your goal. Besides understanding your why, it's another great way to stay motivated.

Action Provoking Exercises and Encouragement

- What is your first money memory?
- What would you want to do if money were no object?
- How much is enough for you today?
- How has it shaped the way think about and handle money today?
- If you were to take the time to write the last chapter of your financial success story, what would we read? Where are you?
- What are you doing?
- What did you accomplish?
- Who is with you?
- How old are you?
- What do you want to be remembered for?
- Where do you live?
- Where did you travel to?
- How many books did you read?
- Who did you help?
- How many businesses did or do you have?
- Did you buy the plane you always wanted?
- Did you take those piano lessons?
- Did you write your book or books?
- Did you get that degree?
- Did you start that charity or charities?
- Did you join that organization?
- Did you maintain that healthy lifestyle?
- Did you buy that vacation property that your family can use whenever they need it?
- Did you paint those portraits?
- Did you take that art class?

- List your possibilities for the next three months.
- How can you make it S.M.A.R.T.Y?
- Under each goal, write out the steps that you will take to achieve your goal.
- How are you planning to celebrate your accomplishment?

What doubtful thought came to mind as you were writing out your success story? What positive affirmation can you write to counteract those beliefs? Commit them to memory or post them in places where you'll see them right away, such as your desk, computer wallpaper, mirror, nightstand, phone wallpaper, etc.

CHAPTER 10

THE CAPACITY TO GIVE

"It is more blessed to give than to receive."

—ACTS 20:35 NLT

Giving is connected to abundance—although this seems counterintuitive. Because after giving, it seems like you have less. However, I have always found that when I give with the proper motives, I feel great. I may have helped someone get through a challenging life moment and by giving I get to experience the joy of watching someone else receive and overcome their challenge. Giving also helps me to pay homage to the people who have given to me. Giving opens us up to receiving more so that we can give more. If I am holding on to something that I can give, then I don't make room to receive. I would call this the circle of giving.

There are some who have no problem giving and others who find that giving will result in them having less. I believe money ebbs and flows. As we consider giving, we're able to take the focus off ourselves and put it on someone or something else.

Giving should be a part of your financial plan no matter where you are. I know that resources can be scarce depending on your situation, but even when they are scarce, it's still good to practice giving. Giving doesn't always have to come in the form of money. It can come in the form of time as well. However, I do believe there is something to be said about consistently allocating a portion of our funds for giving.

I believe giving is a muscle that has to be developed. I usually make sure that at least 10 percent of my income goes to my church in the form of a tithe. You may not go to church; however, it's important to give to a charity of your choice. I love this principle because it allows me to understand that the money in my possession was provided to me by God to manage. Giving puts me in a mindset of gratitude and thankfulness for what I have and takes the focus off what I don't have.

Although not perfect, I have been practicing this for years, pretty much since I attended occasional Sunday school as a little girl. I remember attending the church that my best friend at the time attended. Her mother was our Sunday School teacher that particular day. I must've been in fourth or fifth grade, which means I was nine or ten years old. We had our Sunday School lesson and then the teacher started explaining tithes. When she started explaining that the tithe was 10 percent of our money, my ears perked up. They perked up because I loved math. She proceeded to explain in a very simple fashion how we were to figure out how much to tithe. Once she explained that we take the decimal and move it one place to the left, I was convinced to tithe. Initially, it was a math problem for me. Of course, as I got older, I understood more of the benefits, but I distinctly remember when and where I was when I heard of giving in this manner.

Before I understood tithing, I always remember my mother making sure that we had something to give when the offering plate passed us at church. She wanted to make sure my sisters and I always participated in giving. We weren't giving a percentage of anything in particular, but we knew that the money she gave us was for the purpose of giving and not for buying candy like Now and Laters, Appleheads, or Laffy Taffy, as those purchases were for another time and purpose. When I became an adult and started working, I started this practice consistently and it's always given me hope and contentment even in the midst of hardship.

Even scientists have studied the power of giving. In the article "The Science Behind the Power of Giving" by Jenny Santi, she mentions that "Giving is good for the Giver." "Today, scientific research provides compelling data to support the notion that giving one's time, talents, and treasure is a powerful pathway to finding purpose, transcending difficulties and finding fulfillment and being in life," states Jenny Santi. When neuroscientists Jorge Moll and Jordan Grafman conducted a study with a group of volunteers to observe the brain's response to giving. Grafman and Moll concluded from their experiments that when "the volunteers place the interest of others before their own, the generosity activated a primitive part of the brain that usually lights up in response to food or sex." I have found that many people want to alleviate the stress around money, and I believe giving is one of those acts that will help that happen. We often don't think of giving as part of our financial plan but again, I believe it should be incorporated no matter what your net worth is.

Jaq Campbell

I had the chance to interview Jacqueline "Jaq" Campbell, who has had a successful twenty-seven-year career as a financial advisor and is a leader of financial advisors at a company that managed billions of dollars. She was able to start in the financial services industry in her early twenties. She has a phenomenal story where she decided to pursue her career first and then in later years get her degree. When all her girlfriends graduated high school they went straight to college, and she ended up getting a job. She went the untraditional route but has no regrets, especially since she was able to start her career at an early age. As it turns out, she earned her Bachelor of Arts degree in 2016 from DePaul University at the age of forty years old and graduated debt free by taking advantage of the employee tuition reimbursement program from her employer. Her degree focuses on diversity and inclusion within financial services. Throughout her journey to earning her degree she was able to marry the work she was doing on her job to the work and assignments she completed with her university.

I enjoyed when our conversation turned to the topic of philanthropy. She started giving at an early age as well, and like me, her giving started in the church. She remembers when her church needed to purchase a drum set, and she set out to donate funds to buy them. At that point, she decided that she would be a philanthropist and started to embrace the power of having the philanthropy mindset, which is similar to the giving mindset and opens us up to abundance. When I hear the word philanthropy, used by Jaq to describe her giving, it makes me think of Rockefeller or Gates or Oprah. It conveys to me that the person giving is someone who is "well to do" or "of great means." I liked how she used the word philanthropy to describe her giving because it exudes something greater than one's self and puts you in a wealthy frame of mind.

Regina Alhassan created a TEDxTalk entitled "Money. Black People. Philanthropy." In this talk, she dispels the myth that some people believe Black Americans are not philanthropic. She states that "African Americans are the most charitable group of people in the United States." She shared that according to the Rockefeller Foundation and the Kellogg Foundation, "Nearly two-thirds of African American households donate money to a charity every year." She also shares that "30 percent of African American donors give because of tradition and this number is 18 percent for white households," according to a multi-year study funded by USBank and presented by the US Trust and the Lilly Family School of Philanthropy at Indiana University. It's interesting that she states, "African-American donors are twice as likely to believe in the impact of their gift." Interestingly enough, she also says, "41 percent of African-American donors planned to increase their gift in the next three to five years." With all the bleak statistics on the racial wealth gap, I was happy to see that my people as a whole are rating high in gifting and donations.

I love how Jaq normalizes the word so that it can be embraced by everyday people. She made it her "philanthropic purpose" as she stated to make sure that for every dollar she brings into her household, fifteen cents would go toward philanthropy. She would give to nonprofits, charities, churches, and so on. She decided that her "breakthrough in having a wealthy mindset" was having a philanthropic mindset. She started in her twenties with the drum set, and today she has given close to six figures. Her goal for 2021 is to be able to write a $100,000 check. She really is a believer that giving and philanthropy is a mindset. I am in complete agreement with her statement that "When you choose to be a giver, you will always have money to give."

She gives before she spends money on anything else including food, mortgage, and any other expenses. She says, "That has helped her see blessing after blessing after blessing." Being mindful that she is not only motivated by the blessings that she receives from giving, she also understands that it puts her into a state of abundance. The abundance mindset is important, especially when you consider that we are constantly bombarded with the challenges and struggles of everyday life, whether it's from the TV news programs, online news, or social media. We are constantly hearing about how people are struggling and how much lack there is. The act of giving can help us transcend from a mindset of lack to a mindset of abundance. It takes the focus off ourselves and puts it on others and how we can help others. I love her motto, "Give, Save, Spend, so we can win, win, win." It's important to have a "Give First" mentality.

When I was growing up, my father always told my sisters and me that when we give, it will come back. He made sure we also understood that it may not come back from the place that you gave, but it will come back. This has stuck with me throughout my life. Sometimes when I want to hold back, I have to regroup and engage in giving to get myself out of that rut.

Many are familiar with giving directly to charity or to a friend or to a stranger. However, many do not realize that there is a vehicle called a donor-advised fund, which according to the article entitled "What is a Donor-Advised Fund," is "like a charitable investment account, for the sole purpose of supporting charitable organizations." When one donates to a donor-advised fund, they can receive a tax deduction immediately on the funds deposited into the account. What I find to be really nice about it is that it can be invested for tax-free growth and, whenever you are ready, you can grant the funds to practically any IRS-approved charity. When I first heard about the donor-advised fund, it was referred to as the "poor man's foundation" because it is easier to set up and doesn't have the requirements that many private foundations require. It's a great vehicle to take advantage of a tax deduction and to create a plan for giving and remaining philanthropic. Many charitable arms of brokerage firms like Fidelity, Schwab, and Vanguard offer such accounts (Ebeling 2013). If you are looking to be serious about your giving and make it a part of your overall financial plan, then the donor-advised fund is a great option to take into consideration.

Again, giving takes the focus off ourselves and puts it on others. In recent years, the term "paying it forward" has become very popular. In fact, for several years, the church I belonged to in Phoenix created a "You Just Got Blessed" campaign. It was one where church members would buy groceries, give gift cards, money, or any other creative way to pleasantly surprise a stranger with a gift. It was a lot of fun. I remember purchasing a few gift cards and going about my day seeing who I could walk up to and bless. I think even the process of thinking about this throughout my day was a positive exercise. I also remember being in line at my local grocery store and buying groceries for the person ahead of me. It was wonderful to see the look of surprise on the person's face when I said I'll take care of their bill. Many were shocked. I remember people doing these acts for me over the years, and it always made me feel good to be the receiver as well as the giver. You just never know what someone is going through and how your act of kindness helps them make it through their day.

Often, we associate money with lack or abundance, but at the end of the day, money is a tool to pay bills, to buy something for enjoyment, to give a gift, or even to invest and watch it grow. Once we determine how we want to use our money, we can begin to tell the money what we want it to do rather than have the money be a source of stress and strain. *Time Magazine* shared an article entitled "Being Generous Really Does Make You Happier" regarding the connection between generosity and happiness. The article referred to a study published by *Nature Communications*. The study was conducted by researchers from the University of Zurich in Switzerland. The researchers told fifty people that they'd receive $100. Half the people were to spend the money on themselves, and the other half were asked to spend the money on someone they knew. The researchers wanted to see how the brain responded to pledging generosity and if that made one happier.

They brought everyone into the lab and performed an MRI scan to measure the activity in the three regions of the brain associated with social behavior, generosity, happiness, and decision-making. They asked each person to consider a friend that they wanted to give the gift to and how they imagined spending the money. It was interesting to find that the ones who pledged to give the money away tended to make more generous decisions as opposed to the people who were planning to spend the money on themselves. The ones planning to give the money away initially also had a greater interaction with altruism and happiness. They even reported to have higher levels of happiness after the experiment was over.

Another amazing finding was that according to the lead author of the study, Philippe Tobler, associate professor of neuroeconomics and social neuroscience, "... the amount spent did not matter. It is worth keeping in mind that even little things have a beneficial effect—like bringing coffee to one's office mates in the morning." This is awesome to hear because just as mentioned before from Jaq Campbell you can be a philanthropist at any level of income or net worth. Often, I hear people say they just want peace of mind, security, a stress-free, and a worry-free life when it comes to struggling with finances and the frustrations that arise from it. The simple act of being generous is one of the keys to feeling more happiness according to this research.

In the end of this chapter, I have provided some action-provoking questions for you to answer. It's time to really focus on what matters in our lives. We mustn't let money overtake us to the point that we feel it controls us. We have the opportunity to control money. It is a tool and using it to give and to be philanthropic will help us lead stress-free lives.

Action Provoking Exercise

- When you pass away, what do you want people to say about you and your impact on their lives?
- Honestly assess your giving mindset.
- How does giving make you feel?
- How can you challenge yourself to give more?
- What is enough to give in your mind?
- Do you believe you can be a "philanthropist" now?
- What percentage of your income have you purposed to give on an annual basis?
- In what ways can you give throughout the year to take the focus off yourself and onto others?

CHAPTER 11

COMMUNITY

> "The greatness of community is most accurately measured by the compassionate action of its members."
>
> —CORETTA SCOTT KING

Your "Social Capital"

"Your net worth is tied to your network."

Over the years, I've heard this saying and I believe it to be true. In a previous chapter, I discussed the importance of understanding your personal net worth, which is your assets minus your liabilities. However, numbers tell a story. If you speak with anyone about their net worth, they will be able to tell you how they got there, whether it was an investment purchased, an inheritance, a bankruptcy, or a large loan. There's always a story behind the numbers, which is usually linked to people.

Porter Gale states, "I believe your social capital, or your ability to build a network of authentic personal and professional relationships, not your financial capital, is the most important asset in your portfolio. I believe that seeking out and working in collaboration with others who share your interests and values will provide a stronger foundation, enabling you to reach a higher level of success than you would on your own" (Gale 2013). Calling this your social capital is powerful. I believe creating harmony between your social capital and financial capital allows you to eliminate the selfish pursuit of wealth. It keeps you grounded; it's a fun way to develop relationships along the way and create memories that last a lifetime. Your social capital is all about your relationships and your community.

Turning Struggle into Triumph

Lashea Reaves is a powerful example of the power of community and dispelling the notion that we must pull ourselves up by our own bootstraps. Before I go into how she has embraced community, I will share more about her background after hearing her speak and reading about her life on her non-profit's website. Mrs. Reaves was a product of poverty and saw firsthand the impact financial struggles have on families. At the age of fourteen, she received the gut-wrenching, heartbreaking news that her mother had passed away. It was six days before Christmas. Her mother had died due to hospital negligence. Her father was now a single parent to four daughters. Fortunately, her family won a malpractice lawsuit and a huge settlement. Unfortunately, in less than twenty-four months, the settlement had dwindled to zero, and her family found themselves back on public assistance and living below the poverty line.

Lashea kept pushing forward and decided to enroll at Florida A&M University to create a fresh start for herself. However, by the end of her first year in college she was a homeless single mother. Not only was she struggling to raise her daughter, but her father became sick, and she decided to adopt her younger sister. She anticipated that her father would pass away and decided to take out a student loan to pay for his funeral expenses. Sadly, her father passed away the next year.

With all these life challenges at such a young age, she found herself struggling to provide for her family. Not only was she a struggling college student but she was also a domestic violence survivor. One of her key life turning points was when she was working as a bank teller and decided to share with her boss that she wanted to be a homeowner. Her boss responded with, "Well, what's stopping you?" At this point, she said she realized that "The only limitations in life are the ones we place on ourselves." She experienced a mindset shift and expanded beyond poverty and debt. She decided to manage her finances in a way that aligned with how she wanted to live her life.

As a graduation gift to herself, she purchased her first home. She graduated cum laude with a BS degree in business management. She was off public assistance for the first time in her life and devoured as much as she could about the subject of personal finance. Once she graduated from college, she moved through the ranks at her company at the time, Charles Schwab, becoming an assistant vice president and managing more than $3 billion in assets.

Today, Lashea is the founder of a nonprofit organization located in sunny Orlando, Florida, called "8 Cents in a Jar." This award-winning nonprofit organization was created to

"Ensure future generations have the opportunity to become financially fit regardless of their economic condition." In 2019, 8 Cents in a Jar helped 404 students accumulate savings and wealth totaling $42,932.53. This organization is helping students create generational wealth by community and real-world action (Reaves 2021).

Lashea's story is impactful, and she is using her nonprofit to create a new community for the students who become a part of her organization so that they can live life in a different way. I love how she has taken her struggles and turned them into triumph so that she can help the community around her.

The Need for Trusted Advisors

The power of community is displayed in the form of having trusted advisors. Your advisors are a part of your community. As a fee-only financial planner, I am under obligation to act in the best interest of my clients. I decided to become a fiduciary, which allows me to provide unbiased financial advice. Having a fiduciary financial planner on your team is imperative. In fact, according to a white paper entitled "Two American Financial Plans," "Black families can indeed improve their financial outcomes by adjusting their investment strategy and asset allocation—especially with the advice of financial professionals and financial planners—despite the racial wealth gap's systemic components."

As a CERTIFIED FINANCIAL PLANNER™ professional, besides changing careers in 2004 and gaining valuable work experience, I have gone through training and a rigorous examination, which allows me to provide financial advice in multiple areas for clients seeking financial advice. There are resources by which to search for a fee-only fiduciary financial advisor/planner. Those are the National Association of Personal Financial Advisors, Fee-Only Network, and XY Planning Network. There are lots of professionals that wear the financial advisor title but finding one that is a fiduciary and acts in your best interest is imperative.

Other professionals that are extremely helpful and important to your team are a tax advisor and an estate planning attorney. The tax advisor who can also be a Certified Public Accountant will help you navigate the tax implications of your financial decisions. You want to have an estate planning attorney to help you prepare a will or trust for when you pass away. It is important to utilize professionals in order to know you are tapping into reliable resources.

According to the article "Why the Phrase 'Pull Yourself Up By Your Bootstraps' Is Nonsense," "To pull yourself up by your bootstraps means to succeed or elevate yourself without any outside help." When I think of this term, I know that there is essentially no one who succeeds by themselves. Someone had to help them.

When it comes to the racial wealth gap and its origins, we can see this in full effect. As an example, let's review homesteading in the United States. Since the end of the Civil War, various homestead acts were enacted. At the same time that my ancestors were anticipating forty acres and a mule for their backbreaking free labor to build the United States of America, many Americans who were white and immigrants were given over 246 million acres of western land virtually for free between around 1868 and 1934. It equated to about 160 acres per claimant. So, about 1.5 million white Americans and immigrants received land. Now there were some rules and stipulations around the land and when they could get the deed. But this land was given to them. In the year 2000, it was estimated that forty-six million adult descendants benefited from the various Homestead Acts. Federal policy excluded Black Americans from a legacy of wealth and ownership, and it also perpetuated poverty at the same time. This is just one highlighted aspect of US history and there are countless other historical accounts to provide as examples of this history of economic exclusion (Merritt 2016).

The Praying Grandmother

I am empowered by the stories and know that they give us encouragement and help us to understand we can't do this alone. I am reminded of the story of Eddie Brown who is the founder of Brown Capital Management. Brown was born in Apopka, Florida, a city outside of Orlando, Florida, to a thirteen-year-old mother. He was mostly reared by his grandmother and his grandfather. In his town, Black and white people were separated by railroad tracks and being that this was considered Jim Crow South, you knew never to cross those tracks.

Eddie always had a love for education. At a young age, his grandmother would show him another side of life, opposing the life of back-breaking labor that she and her husband did. He remembers her taking him to the "Big City," Orlando, and showing him men in suits behind a desk. Then she'd say, "Little Eddie Carl, if you stay in school, study hard, and do well, you too, one day, can sit behind a desk and with a white shirt and tie." His grandmother gave him a vision and an aspiration of something that was better than what he saw everyone else doing around him. Brown saw that vision come true once he changed from being an electrical engineer to financial services professional, he served as a portfolio manager for ten years at T. Rowe Price before starting his own firm in 1983. T. Rowe Price was established in 1937 and in 1973 Eddie became the first Black professional ever hired by the company.

Remarkably, he never felt like he was "different" in his work environment. He said he just felt like a portfolio manager "working with the team and the group." He learned that team-based work can be more efficient than individual-based work and he decided that when he started his own business it would be from a team-based approach.

Brown and his wife, Sylvia, are active philanthropists in Baltimore, Maryland. He and his wife created a family foundation under the umbrella of the Baltimore Community foundation to address and improve the education outcomes for Black students in Baltimore. An additional need they saw was in healthcare for the Black community; his wife served on the Advisory Board of the Bloomberg School of Public Health at Johns Hopkins University. Due to this health disparity, he learned that the life expectancy difference between the most affluent sections of Baltimore city and the poorest sections is more than twenty years. Eddie and Sylvia have two daughters and three grandsons, and they are creating a legacy of multi-generational philanthropy to continue to make change for the Baltimore community.

Eddie Brown recommends the following to young entrepreneurs who would like to follow in his footsteps: "Make sure you have the right educational background for what you're thinking about doing. Get some experience, preferably, on someone else's payroll. Have a great viable big idea that you think is viable to gain opportunity. Then, get capital, preferably, without debt. Make sure you can maintain the lifestyle that you and your family are used to. Take calculated risk. Make sure you have a spouse that can be supportive" (CNBCAfrica 2019).

Eddie Brown's is another powerful story that we must have a community to help us make it. Whether it's a praying grandmother that speaks life, a boss that provides an encouraging word, or a teacher that takes the time to help you learn a new subject. It all takes community. No one makes these strides in a vacuum.

Leveraging Community

Jean Brownhill is a trained architect and the founder of a company called Sweeten, as in "home sweet home." Sweeten was founded in 2011 after she painstakingly attempted to renovate her own Brooklyn townhouse. Sweeten uses technology to unite homeowners with vetted contractors to help make the renovation process saner, smoother, and more transparent with advice at no additional cost to the homeowner. Jean Brownhill is one of the few Black female entrepreneurs to raise over $1 million in venture capital.

Today, Sweeten has more than $1 billion in its pipeline for commercial and residential projects. Sweeten is a service based in New York City and it's offered in many cities across the US.

Jean is a catalyst for leveraging community. Because she works with contractors and they are usually forgotten, she says that Sweeten's competitive advantage is that they respect and listen to their contractors by creating tools based on their feedback. By simply joining Sweeten's network, contractors are able to take their business that generates about $500,000 per year to $3 to $4 million per year. They take on a lot of the back-end support for the contractors and help them to grow to where they aspire to be (Business of Home 2020). It's a win-win, and Jean's business embodies the power of community and building relationships to help everyone thrive financially.

Action Provoking Activity

- Who has been instrumental in helping you get to where you are today?
- What community or support do you need to tap into to reach your goals?
- How will you focus on building your social capital and your financial capital (net worth)?

CONCLUSION

Your dreams and your vision matter. With God, all things are possible. When I started writing this book, I didn't realize that the horrible Tulsa Race Massacre would commemorate its one-hundred-year anniversary in the midst of my editing process. I don't believe this is a coincidence. I just knew that the story needed to constantly be shared. I knew that I come from a line of strong independent, hard-working ancestors who paved the way for me. I understood that economic injustice must be served for the descendants of Greenwood, other communities, and the descendants of enslaved Africans in America. I knew that if we can expose and get economic justice and reparations for the survivors and descendants of Greenwood, soon we'd have a roadmap for reparations for all descendants of enslaved Africans in America.

I knew that there has been a history of systemic racism and economic exclusion in America that strives to keep Black Americans, whose ancestors built this country under duress, toil, and strain, down economically under the false pretense that "Everyone else came to this country and 'made it' why can't you?" I want this country to not only recognize the injustices done to my community mentally, physically, and economically but to also repair what has been done. Yes, it baffles me that the US has decided to ignore this part of our history by not approving reparations when the US provided reparations for other ethnic groups.

I still have hope, however. My motto is to always have hope, for it's the priceless currency for getting through life. My ancestors dug deep to thrive and survive despite their pain and suffering. Their faith in God and relentless hope is why I am here today. I must continue to have hope. Because of my hope and faith in God, I believe that one day economic justice will be served.

In the meantime, my desire is to continue to challenge you and those in my community to ask the question, "How can I?" I want the stories of the inspiring people in this book to create hope and spark creativity for answering the question, "How can I?"—especially until that long overdue day when I and my people get reparations. I know that in this country of the "American Dream" there are people who are still overcoming and breaking generational curses. I want the stories to help create that "super" community and encourage you to nurture your own special community of people to surround yourself with people who are focused on economic well-being so that you are held accountable and stay motivated to create your own narrative of what financial freedom looks like for you and your family. I want the financial education activities in the book to create "Action Provoking" implementation of concepts and ideas to generate wealth and promote economic empowerment against all odds.

I want you to understand the power of measuring your wealth, building assets instead of debt, investing, creating S.M.A.R.T.Y. possibilities, building your emergency fund, passing on wealth and protecting your wealth. I want you to understand how the power of giving enhances our lives and takes the focus off ourselves and what we may or may not have. I want people to focus on living and maximizing our God-given talents and abilities. I want us to share information with others and support others' ideas with encouraging words and our resources. I want us to feel empowered to create and innovate because the question "How can I?" challenges us to understand that there's always a way, there's always a solution and that no matter what, we can achieve it if we believe it. We have to embrace that the race is not given to the swift but to those who endure to the end. Continue to endure.

RESOURCES

At the end of each chapter there are Action Provoking Activities. Due to limited space, I have created a Companion Workbook for you to download for free. Please visit bit.ly/ysfabookresource to download it today.

ACKNOWLEDGMENTS

Thanks to all my supporters of this book project and book journey. I sincerely appreciate those who became early readers and shared your feedback. To all my family, friends, colleagues, and supporters, I graciously appreciate you. Thanks be to God.

Bri Adams, Richard Aldridge, Eunice Allen, Rashid Alsabur, Tawana Ansah, Adewunmi Ashaye, Henry Qawi Austin, Sylvia M Badie, Tyree Bailey, Maria Bailey-Benson, Arlene Blake, Marlyn Bonzil-Juste, Walter K Booker, Lazetta Braxton, Welby Broaddus, Donte' Brock, Nadia Brown, Rockisha D. Brown, Melvin Brown, Dawnara Brown, Jeffrey Byas, Theresa C. Campbell, Rich Carroll, Gabriella Cerezo, Dr. Preston D. Cherry, Kimberly Clark, Isha Cogborn, Genoah Collins, Julia Collins, Jerome E. Crawford II, Sally Cummins, Richard Cuvilly, C. Kenneth Davidson II, Felicia Davis, Anna Dawson, Makkeda Deloney, Hedia E. Diawara, Tina Diggs, Janice Dudley, Stephanie Felder, LaReesa Ferdinand-Dukes, Shawna and Patrick Flythe, Kellee Ford, Zel Fowler, Tanya Frias, Melissa Geter, Michael Gibson, Valencia Gibson, Scott

Gill, Marcelline Girlie, Erica Glaze, Equisha Glenn, Tracy and Jeff Glover, Nicole Goodwin, Rita Grant, Albaney Gray, Shalonda Gray, Tasha Gray, Tyra Green, Alethea Greene, Nermin Hadzihasanovic, Kimberly Hamiter, Tangi Herndon, Nicole Hill-Eugene, Janina Hogans, Olivea Holley, Tenise Hordge, Judia Jackson, Rhonda Peters James, Jennifer Jasper, Carmen Johnson, Nicole Johnson, La'Vista Jones, Hope Kiriisa, Anne Kirkham, Eric Koester, La Tonya Lawrence, Kellee Leandre, Michael and Jolene LeFlore, Lisa, Dawn R. Littlejohn, Anika M. Mack, Lora Mariner, Sefa Mawuli, Dr. Jackie Mayfield, Gretchen McCrae, Larry McCullum, Oriel McKinney, Clarissa Mitchell, Chloe Moore, Kathryn Morris, Elsie Muhammad, Antoinette Munroe, Zarinah Nadir, Cady North, Pascal and Angelica Ouandji, Kiya Patrick, Karen Pelot, James Perdue, Scott Perrone, Lamyai Phaxay-Kizzee, Begoña Pino, Kirk Poole, Kendra Prince, Renee Ray, Carmen Ray, Renzo Reyes, Cameo Roberson, Jacqueline Robinson, Luis Rosa, Renee Perdue Rucker, Jan Schalk, Karenna Senors, Donna Sewell, William T. Shepard Jr., William Shepard, Demetria H. Sloan, Linda Joyce Smallwood, Paula J. Smallwood, Lennie Smallwood, Harry and Debra Smallwood, Reshell Smith, Sherrye Smith, Jang Smith, Pam Smith, Robin Spencer, Jennifer St. Clair, Stacy Stark, Fara Sue, Shelva Suggs, Kendra Tillman, Octavia Tillman, Anissa W. Tolliver, Michelle Traveler, Cynthia Tucker, Lisa Turner, Kimberly Varnado, Demetria Wade, Tee-Ta Walker, Cynthia Weaver, Herbert White, Patricia Whorton, Linda Marie Williams, Linda Marie Williams, Jennifer Williams, Roslyn Williams, Mia Wood, Kathleen and Willie Wooten, Sean Wooten, Sirah Waazor Yaakpogoro, Joan Young

APPENDIX

Introduction

Astor, Maggie. "What to Know About the Tulsa Greenwood Massacre." *NY Times,* June 20, 2020. https://www.nytimes.com/2020/06/20/us/tulsa-greenwood-massacre.html.

Black Wall Street USA. https://blackwallstreetusa.wixsite.com/blackwallstreetusa.

Clark, Alexis. "Tulsa's 'Black Wall Street' Flourished as a Self-Contained Hub in Early 1900s." *History Channel,* January 27, 2021. https://www.history.com/news/black-wall-street-tulsa-race-massacre.

Energy HQ. "TULSA: OIL CAPITAL OF THE WORLD AND THRIVING METROPOLIS." May 2017. https://energyhq.com/2017/05/tulsa-oil-capital-of-the-world-and-thriving-metropolis/.

Gara, Antoine. "The Bezos of Black Wall Street." *Forbes,* June 18, 2020. https://www.forbes.com/sites/antoinegara/2020/06/18/the-bezos-of-black-wall-street-tulsa-race-riots-1921/?sh=6e1c27bdf321.

Henderson, Brooke. "Meet the Entrepreneur Who Created the First 'Black Wall Street.'" *Inc. Magazine,* December 1, 2020. https://www.inc.com/magazine/202011/brooke-henderson/o-w-gurley-tulsa-oklahoma-business-black-wall-street.html.

Merrefield, Clark. "The 1921 Tulsa Race Massacre and the Financial Fallout." *The Harvard Gazette,* June 18, 2020. https://news.harvard.edu/gazette/story/2020/06/the-1921-tulsa-race-massacre-and-its-enduring-financial-fallout/

Montford, Christina. "6 Interesting Things You Didn't Know About 'Black Wall Street.'" *Atlanta Black Star,* December 2, 2014. https://atlantablackstar.com/2014/12/02/6-interesting-things-you-didnt-know-about-black-wall-street/.

Moreno, Carlos. "The Victory of Greenwood O. W. Gurley." *New Tulsa Star,* December 23, 2019. https://newtulsastar.com/2019/12/23/the-victory-of-greenwood-o-w-gurley/.

Morrison, Aaron. "100 Years after the Tulsa Race Massacre, The Damage Remains." *AP News,* May 25, 2021. https://apnews.com/article/tulsa-race-massacre-1921-100-years-later-3bc13e842c31054a90b6d1c81db9d70c.

Rao, Sameer. "Remember the Tulsa 'Black Wall Street' Massacre Through Its Last Known Survivor." *Colorlines,* June 1, 2018. https://www.colorlines.com/articles/remember-tulsa-black-wall-street-massacre-through-its-last-known-survivor.

"The Tulsa Race Massacre." *Oklahoma Historical Society,* Accessed June 18, 2021. https://www.okhistory.org/learn/trm5.

"You Dropped a Bomb on Me." *Song Facts®,* Accessed June 18, 2021. https://www.songfacts.com/facts/the-gap-band/you-dropped-a-bomb-on-me.

Section 1: Build

Kiddie Encyclopedia. "Nutrient Facts for Kids." April 14, 2021. https://kids.kiddle.co/Nutrient.

Chapter 1: Values

Bellard, David and Jalen Clark. "EP 66—Walking in Your Purpose (Guest: Raven Magwood)." June 29, 2020. *Black Wealth Renaissance*, Podcast, MP3 Audio, 38:14. https://podcasts.apple.com/us/podcast/ep-66-walking-in-your-purpose-guest-raven-magwood/id1456152559?i=1000480166284.

Brook, Alyssa. "Raven Magwood Shows What It Takes to Be a Million-Dollar Businesswoman." *Hollywood Unlocked*, May 29, 2019. https://hollywoodunlocked.com/raven-magwood-shows-what-it-takes-to-be-a-million-dollar-businesswoman/.

Gaetano, Chris. "Survey: 77 Percent of Americans Stressed Over Finances." *NYS Society of CPAs*, January 28, 2020. https://www.nysscpa.org/news/publications/nextgen/nextgen-article/survey-77-percent-of-americans-stressed-over-finances-012820.

Luscombe, Belinda. "Do We Need $75,000 a Year to Be Happy?" *Time Magazine*, September 6, 2010. http://content.time.com/time/magazine/article/0,9171,2019628,00.html.

Pullum, Roderick. "Before We Tell You About a Release, Let Us Explain What a Cypher Is in Hip-Hop." *Dallas Observer,* May 24, 2019. https://www.dallasobserver.com/music/we-looked-into-the-origin-of-the-word-cypher-in-hip-hop-11670485.

TEDx Talks. "Born to Move the Crowd: Rha Goddess at TEDxBroadStreet." November 19, 2013. Video, 16:38. https://youtu.be/FCC-jEgWEWA.

Chapter 2: Tenacity

Arian Simone. "Arian Simone's Fearless Journey." January 30, 2012. Video, 12:03. https://youtu.be/I5zsq5BemZM.

Earn Your Leisure. "14-Year-Old Ceo Retires His Mom." April 7, 2020. Video, 1:09:00. https://youtu.be/9_MDty-oXeI.

In the Know. "This 13-year-old fashion designer is on a mission to make his clothing line a household name." January 19, 2020. Video, 5:42. https://youtu.be/fuFCtdGyINQ.

The Ellen Show. "'Best. News. Ever.': Sean 'Diddy' Combs and Jeannie Surprise Deserving Fan Trey Brown." June 29, 2020. Video, 5:43. https://youtu.be/uoZ1x_foPVE.

Chapter 3: Net Worth

Asante-Muhammad, Dedrick, Chuck Collins, Josh Hoxie, and Emanuel Nieves. "The Road to Zero Wealth." *Prosperity Now*, September 2017. https://prosperitynow.org/files/PDFs/road_to_zero_wealth.pdf.

Bundrick, CFP®, Hal M. and Max Ramirez. "Net Worth Calculator: Find Your Net Worth." *NerdWallet*, October 8, 2020. https://www.nerdwallet.com/article/finance/net-worth-calculator.

Garcia, Jose. "The Color of Debt: Credit Card Debt by Race and Ethnicity Fact Sheet." *Demos*, August 31, 2010. https://www.demos.org/policy-briefs/color-debt-credit-card-debt-race-and-ethnicity.

Kelly, Robert. "Wealth." *Investopedia*, August 25, 2021. https://www.investopedia.com/terms/w/wealth.asp#:~:text=What%20Is%20Wealth%3F,owned%2C%20then%20subtracting%20all%20debts.

"Why Does a New Car Lose Value After It's Driven Off the Lot?" *CarsDirect*, March 11, 2020. https://www.carsdirect.com/used-car-prices/why-does-a-new-car-lose-value-after-its-driven-off-the-lot.

Williamson, Vanessa "Closing the Racial Wealth Gap Requires Heavy, Progressive Taxation of Wealth." *Brookings*, December 9, 2020. https://www.brookings.edu/research/closing-the-racial-wealth-gap-requires-heavy-progressive-taxation-of-wealth/.

Section 2: Live

"Brain Twister: What does 1 Trillion Look Like?" *The Dispatch*, August 3, 2019. https://www.the-dispatch.com/photogallery/NC/20190803/NEWS/803009984/PH/1.

Fernando, Jason. "Gross Domestic Product." *Investopedia*, April 25, 2021. https://www.investopedia.com/terms/g/gdp.asp.

Silver, Caleb. "The Top 25 Economies in the World" *Investopedia*, December 24, 2020. https://www.investopedia.com/insights/worlds-top-economies/#1-united-states.

Chapter 4: The Better Rainy Days—Savings and Emergency Fund

Corley, Tom. "Author Who Studies Millionaires: How to Create Wealth Like the Rich." *CNBC*, November 27, 2018. https://www.cnbc.com/2018/11/27/tom-corley-create-wealth-like-the-rich-with-multiple-income-streams.html.

Chapter 5: Protect Your Wealth: Are you on Team "Bounce My Last Check"?

"The Faces and Facts of Disability." *Social Security.* https://www.ssa.gov/disabilityfacts/facts.html.

Egan, John and Amy Danise. "Survey Exposes Gaps in Black Ownership of Life Insurance." *Forbes Advisor*, November 2, 2020. https://www.forbes.com/advisor/life-insurance/black-ownership/.

Jackson, Anna-Louise. "Over Half of Americans Saving for Retirement Make a Money Mistake You Can Fix in Just 3 Minutes." *Grow*, October 22, 2019. https://grow.acorns.com/update-your-beneficiaries/.

Jones, Janelle. "Receiving an Inheritance Helps White Families More Than Black Families." *Economic Policy Institute*, February 17, 2017. https://www.epi.org/publication/receiving-an-inheritance-helps-white-families-more-than-black-families/.

Kagan, Julia. "Trust." *Investopedia*, October 19, 2020. https://www.investopedia.com/terms/t/trust.asp.

Rotter, Kimberly. "Power of Attorney: When You Need One." *Investopedia*, April 30, 2021. https://www.investopedia.com/articles/personal-finance/101514/power-attorney-do-you-need-one.asp.

Medine, Taylor. "Is There a Life Insurance Race Gap?" *Haven Life (blog)*, September 24, 2020. https://havenlife.com/blog/life-insurance-racial-wealth-gap-statistics/.

Rose, Georgia. "Discriminatory Practices Leave Black Americans with Less Life Insurance." *NerdWallet*, February 8, 2021. https://www.nerdwallet.com/article/insurance/african-american-life-insurance.

Smith, Lisa. "What Is a Will and Why Do I Need One Now?" *Investopedia*, April 10, 2021. https://www.investopedia.com/articles/pf/08/what-is-a-will.asp.

Swarns, Rachel. "Insurance Policies on Slaves: New York Life's Complicated Past." *The New York Times*, December 18, 2016. https://www.nytimes.com/2016/12/18/us/insurance-policies-on-slaves-new-york-lifes-complicated-past.html.

Section 3: Save

Chan, Pamela, and Spectra Myers. "Overdue: Addressing Debt in Black Communities." *Prosperity Now*, August 2018. https://prosperitynow.org/resources/addressing-debt-black-communities.

Nieves, Emanuel. "What We've Learned About Debt in Black Communities." *Prosperity Now (Blog)*, February 7, 2019. https://prosperitynow.org/blog/what-weve-learned-about-debt-black-communities.

Chapter 6: Don't Put All Your Money in One Bucket

Sunstein, Cass R., Richard H. Thaler. *Nudge: Improving Decisions about Health, Wealth, and Happiness*. New York: Penguin Books, 2008.

Chapter 7: Owe No Man—From Debt Management to Debt Elimination

Barone, Adam. "How Credit Card Balance Transfers Work." Investopedia, May 4, 2021. https://www.investopedia.com/credit-cards/balance-transfer-credit-card/.

"Get My Free Credit Report." *Federal Trade Commission*, Accessed May 23, 2021. https://www.ftc.gov/faq/consumer-protection/get-my-free-credit-report.

Irby, Latoya. "Why Credit Card Companies Target College Students." *the balance,* March 20, 2021. https://www.thebalance.com/credit-card-companies-love-college-students-960090.

Kagan, Julia. "Lifestyle Creep." *Investopedia,* November 29, 2020. https://www.investopedia.com/terms/l/lifestyle-creep.asp.

O'Shea, Bev and Sean Pyles. "How to Use Debt Avalanche." *Nerdwallet,* April 23, 2021. https://www.nerdwallet.com/article/finance/what-is-a-debt-avalanche.

Single Care (Blog) "2021 Medical Debt Statistics." January 4, 2021. https://www.singlecare.com/blog/medical-debt-statistics/.

Chapter 8: Start with What You Have

Bhutta, Neil, Andrew C. Chang, Lisa J. Dettling, and Joanne W. Hsu. "Disparities in Wealth by Race and Ethnicity in the 2019 Survey of Consumer Finances." *Federal Reserve*, September 28, 2020. https://www.federalreserve.gov/econres/notes/feds-notes/disparities-in-wealth-by-race-and-ethnicity-in-the-2019-survey-of-consumer-finances-20200928.htm.

Boyd, Herb. "BLACK HISTORY MONTH 2016: Slaves Were Bought and Sold on Wall Street in New York City in 1711." *New York*

Daily News, February 11, 2016. https://www.nydailynews.com/new-york/slaves-bought-sold-wall-street-1711-article-1.2526003.

Koval, Margaret. *She Roars* podcast talks to Mellody Hobson, a national leader on financial literacy who will receive top alumni award." *Princeton University,* February 22, 2019. https://www.princeton.edu/news/2019/02/22/she-roars-podcast-talks-mellody-hobson-national-leader-financial-literacy-who-will.

Ludlow, Ed, Jonathan Roeder, and Bloomberg. "Starbucks Names Mellody Hobson as Board Chair in Push to Diversify Company Leadership." *Fortune,* December 9, 2020. https://fortune.com/2020/12/09/starbucks-mellody-hobson-board-chair-black-directors/.

TEDxYouth. "Financial Literacy: Mellody Hobson at TEDxMidwest." March 11, 2014. Video, 16:03. https://youtu.be/h905Zx7m4Fs.

"The Great Migration." *History.com,* January 26, 2021. https://www.history.com/topics/black-history/great-migration.

Thomas, Zoe. "The Hidden Links Between Slavery and Wall Street." *BBC,* August 29, 2019. https://www.bbc.com/news/business-49476247.

"How Much Do I Need to Retire?" *Fidelity Viewpoints,* July 21, 2020. https://www.fidelity.com/viewpoints/retirement/how-much-do-i-need-to-retire.

https://www.cnbc.com/select/savings-by-age/.

"The Theory of the Leisure Class: An Economic Study in the Evolution of Institutions." Bright Side Bookshop. https://www.brightsidebookshop.com/book/9782382747599.

Section 4: Give

Newland, Stephen. "The Power of Accountability." *The Standard Newsletter*, 3rd Quarter 2018. https://www.afcpe.org/news-and-publications/the-standard/2018-3/the-power-of-accountability/.

Chapter 9: Your Financial Success Story

Cardinal Health. "About Us.", Accessed June 4, 2021. https://www.cardinalhealth.com/en/about-us.html.

Elliott, CFP®, Kamila, Brent Kessel, CFP®, and Ako Ndefop-Haven. *Two American Financial Plans*. Accessed June 19, 2021. https://theracialwealthgap.com/.

Oliver, Brittney. "The Hidden "Black Tax" That Some Professionals of Color Struggle With." *FastCompany*, February 5, 2019. https://www.fastcompany.com/90296371/the-hidden-black-tax-that-some-professionals-of-color-struggle-with.

Chapter 10: The Capacity to Give

Ebeling, Ashlea. "The Hottest Way to Give to Charity." *Forbes*, November 12, 2013. https://www.fidelitycharitable.org/guidance/philanthropy/what-is-a-donor-advised-fund.html.

Macmillan, Amanda. "Being Generous Really Does Make You Happier." *TIME*. July 14, 2017. https://time.com/4857777/generosity-happiness-brain/.

Santi, Jenny. "The Science Behind the Power of Giving (Op-Ed)." *Live Science*, May 21, 2021. https://www.livescience.com/52936-need-to-give-boosted-by-brain-science-and-evolution.html.

TEDx Talks. "Money. Black People. Philanthropy. | Regina Alhassan | TEDxKingLincolnBronzeville." December 9, 2019. Video, 15:46. https://youtu.be/kuQGYNlEJgU.

"What is a Donor-Advised Fund?" *Fidelity Charitable.* https://www.fidelitycharitable.org/guidance/philanthropy/what-is-a-donor-advised-fund.html.

Chapter 11: Community

Bologna, Caroline. "Why the Phrase 'Pull Yourself Up by Your Bootstraps' Is Nonsense." *Huffpost*, August 9, 2018. https://m.huffpost.com/us/entry/us_5b1ed024e4b0bbb7a0e037d4.

Business of Home. "The Future of On-Demand Design with Jean Brownhill and Alessandra Wood." July 7, 2020, Video, 36:18. https://youtu.be/cL3aFzpo5Mo.

CNBCAfrica. "My Worst Day: One on One with Eddie Brown Founder of Brown Capital Management." August 8, 2019, Video, 28:04. https://youtu.be/AzQfF1Fk_Cc.

Elliott, CFP®, Kamila, Brent Kessel, CFP®, and Ako Ndefop-Haven. *Two American Financial Plans.* Accessed June 19, 2021. https://theracialwealthgap.com/.

Gale, Porter. "Why Your Network Is Your Net Worth." *Huffpost,* August 3, 2013. https://www.huffpost.com/entry/why-your-network-is-your-_b_3375954.

Merritt, Keri Leigh. "Land and the Roots of African-American Poverty." *Aeon Newsletter,* March 11, 2016. https://aeon.co/ideas/land-and-the-roots-of-african-american-poverty.

Reaves, Lashea. "(Her) story of 8 Cents." *8 Cents in a Jar,* Accessed May 30, 2021. https://www.8cents.org/about.

www.ingramcontent.com/pod-product-compliance
Lightning Source LLC
LaVergne TN
LVHW011831060526
838200LV00053B/3971